LARRY LETOURNEAU   "97"

MARTYR OF BROTHERLY LOVE

Father Engelmar Unzeitig, C.M.M., 1911–1945.

Martyr of Brotherly Love

Father Engelmar Unzeitig and the Priests' Barracks at Dachau

ADALBERT L. BALLING, C.M.M.,
and REINHARD ABELN

Translated by Vergil Heier, C.M.M.

CROSSROAD • NEW YORK

1992
The Crossroad Publishing Company
370 Lexington Avenue, New York, NY 10017

Originally published as *Speichen am Rad der Zeit: Pater Engelmar Unzeitig und der Priesterblock im KZ Dachau*
© Verlag Herder Freiburg im Briesgau 1985

Translation copyright © 1992 by the Congregation of Mariannhill Missionaries

Printed in the United States of America

Library of Congress Cataloging-in-Publication Data

Balling, Adalbert Ludwig.
   [Speichen am Rad der Zeit. English]
   Martyr of brotherly love : Father Engelmar Unzeitig and the
priests' barracks at Dachau / Adalbert L. Balling and Reinhard Abeln
; translated by Vergil Heier.
     p. cm.
   Includes bibliographical references and index.
   ISBN 0-8245-1216-2
   1. Unzeitig, Engelmar, 1911–1945. 2. Catholic Church—Clergy—
Biography. 3. Catholic Church—Germany—History—1933–1945.
4. Dachau (Germany : Concentration camp) I. Abeln, Reinhard.
II. Title.
BX4705.U5259B3513   1992
282'.092—dc20
[B]   92-18479
                                       CIP

CONTENTS

CONTENTS

PREFACE

*"When sin overflowed, so did grace.
When guilt grew, so did love."*
                    Auxiliary Bishop
                Joseph Buchkremer, Aachen

In 1945, a frightful war came to an end, thus concluding miserably the twelve-year atheistic dictatorship of Adolf Hitler. Indescribable misery, unspeakable bodily and spiritual suffering came upon Germany, Europe, and all the peoples afflicted by the war due to the terror of National Socialism (Nazism).

What evil and inhuman things happened through the Nazi leaders will never be completely grasped, never completely revealed, whatever films or books will be written. That is especially true of the concentration camps, those "terrible death factories" (Walter Nigg). Nowhere as in the concentration camps did those in power show their true face, whether those camps stood in Auschwitz, Bergen-Belsen, Buchenwald, Flossenbürg, Majdanek, Mauthausen, Notzweiler or in Neuengamme, Ravensbrück, Sachsenhausen, Stutthoff, Theresienstadt, Treblinka, and Dachau.

All the concentration camps were horrible and inhuman. (All told, there were twenty-seven concentration camps, with 329 larger, affiliated camps in Middle Europe, not counting the camps in Greece, Italy, Yugoslavia, and Norway.) They were meant in the first place to separate, defame, debase, and also break, especially spiritually, the enemies of the Nazis and thereby "neutralize" them. The television series *Holocaust* and *Playing for Time* (about the women's orchestra in Auschitz) were depressing tragedies about the situation in the concentration camps, but they were only partial scenes. The reality was infinitely more horrible.

Not two months after Hitler's "coming into power," the first concentration camp in Germany was set up in Dachau. It became the model of violence and inhumanity, the epitome of all concentration camps. More than 200,000 prisoners from nearly forty nations were registered there. Among them were many clergymen: Catholic (almost 3,000 in number), Orthodox, and Protestant. Their human dignity was literally trampled all over in this camp (in the so-called priests' barracks, which were barracks Nos. 26 and 28).

One of the Catholic priests was the Mariannhill Missionary Father Engelmar Unzeitig. He passed four of his six years as a priest in the Dachau concentration camp. Priests who were in the concentration camp call him the "German Maximilian Kolbe," occasionally also the "Angel of Dachau" or the "Martyr of Brotherly Love." Father Engelmar volunteered to care for the prisoners with typhus shortly before the end of the war. He himself caught the disease and died on March 2, 1945, only weeks before the liberation of Dachau by the Americans. His volunteering was a conscious going to his death. Without regard for his health, quietly and with resignation, yet full of vitality for the Kingdom of God, Father Engelmar helped those who could no longer help themselves. In the name of the Lord, he burned himself out for his sick brothers and offered them his life. The motto of his action was the words of Saint John: "No one has greater love than he who lays down his life for his friends" (Jn 15:13).

This book tells the story of Father Engelmar's life and death; it shows how very much life for this quiet and inconspicuous Mariannhill priest meant ultimately service of his neighbor, a service in the service of God. At the same time, this volume will tell about many other clergymen who spent long years of their lives in the Dachau concentration camp, who by their suffering and dying gave witness to the dignity of human beings and to the God of life, to whom they entrusted themselves, who "by being put through the mill, broken completely, ground into porridge, could not but give off sweetness" (Helder Camara).

In addition, this book reports (only partially, of course) about the Dachau concentration camp, life in the camp, the inhuman conditions and the vexations of the SS. The descriptions—in the beginning and then scattered in the following chapters—are far less than the reality. Suffering and pain, in the last analysis, cannot be grasped in words nor put down in statistics. Nevertheless, they should show that never and in no other place were such satanically brutal executioners at work as in Hitler's liquidation camps.

The poet Ernst Wiechert wrote in 1939(!) about his experience in the Buchenwald concentration camp: "I only stood at the gate and looked upon the dark stage. . . . But the spokes of the terrible wheel had begun to turn already, and blood and horror dripped out of its shining circle."

Spokes of the terrible wheel—that was everyone, once they were caught up in the SS machine. Spokes on the wheel of time.

It was not possible to protect or defend oneself. To resist would have meant death. Everyone knew it. It was just as clear to the priests in Dachau as to the inmates of Auschwitz or any of the other concentration camps.

This book is a revised and abridged version of Adalbert Balling's book *Einer Spur der Liebe hinterlassen: Pater Engelmar (Hubert) Unzeitig, 1911–1945, Mariannhiller Missionar, Märtyrer der Nächstenliebe im KZ Dachau* (Missionsverlag Mariannhill, Würzburg/Reimlingen 1984). Whoever, therefore, wants more information about Father Engelmar, the suffering and death of his fellow prisoners, as well as the inhuman conditions in the Dachau concentration camp during the time of the Nazis, should get hold of this detailed biography.

1

DACHAU—MAN-MADE HELL

Dachau—a "fresh, happy, and laughing place" (Lorenz Westenrieder) with a wonderful castle, old bourgeois houses, and the most beautiful baroque hall north of the Alps! The 1,200-year-old-city before the gates of Munich. The largest German artist colony at the turn of the century.

The Dachau of the modern tourist literature is not the Dachau of the days of the Nazi regime. For the people of Dachau also suffer from this nightmare. "Their good name the people of Dachau earned in their centuries-long history; their bad name was forced upon them by a criminal system," writes Dr. Lorenz Reitmeier, mayor of this large county capital in Bavaria. "Dachau became a negative symbol. The worldwide admiration of this once large artists' colony has long since given way to the terrible inferno."

Hitler's rule of terror ended in 1945. The shudder over the name of Dachau has continued partly even to this day. The Nazi "mark of Cain" will remain with this city for a long time. Dachau is the place where, since March 1933, the infamous concentration camp has stood in which hundreds of thousands of people, herded together, lived and slaved, and where many of them died.

Barracks City and SS Headquarters

The concentration camp of Dachau was a rectangle about 300 meters wide and 600 meters long. To the west of it was the SS camp. It was much more spaciously laid out than the barracks city of the prisoners, with wide asphalt streets, about two hundred and fifty buildings including hospitals, clothing warehouses, the infamous SS leadership school, Himmler's personal staff building, barracks for the SS, innumerable factories for the production of weapons, china, and equipment of every kind, training shops, offices, post office, registry office, amusement facilities, theater, cinema, officers' mess, playing fields, swimming pool, living quarters for the families of the SS, and so on.

This SS city, immediately next to the concentration camp, had been erected with the help of cheap prison labor. A wide street led from the SS "military camp" to the prison camp. At the end of the street was the administration building, also called the Jourhaus, with entrance to the concentration camp. On the metal grate above the entrance stood the motto *Arbeit Macht Frei* ("Work Frees").

The real concentration camp (on the right side of the Wurm Creek) was surrounded by high walls and rolls of electrified barbed wire. An eye could be kept on the whole terrain from high watch towers. The SS were on guard day and night. At night, huge floodlights shined on the barracks. Patrols with watchdogs continually circled the camp, which in addition was surrounded by a moat as well as a path for the patrols next to the "death strip," an area where anyone who stepped into it was shot usually without warning.

The seven watch towers were so placed that there were no hidden corners in the entire camp and every inch could be reached by the machine guns. "In fact, no one ever escaped directly from the camp. The few escapes were from work groups outside of the camp" (R. Schnabel, *Die Frommen in der Hölle*). On the south side within the walls and barbed wire stood the so-called business buildings: kitchen, laundry, shower rooms, clothing warehouses, blacksmith shop, shoe shop, sock mending shop, typewriter repair shop, bunker (also for "fallen" SS personnel), and so on.

To the right and left of the large camp street stood seventeen barracks on each side. These were the quarters of the prisoners. In the first buildings (barracks) were the offices for arranging the work, the camp writing room, the library, and mess hall as well as rooms for the "officials" and employees of the various workshops. The infirmary (barracks for the sick) was lodged in the first five or six barracks, depending on the number of patients. The barracks on the left side had even numbers, the ones on the right odd numbers.

The priests' barracks—we will have very much to write about them—were Barracks 26 and 28. Next to Barracks 29 was the rabbit farm (with about four thousand chinchillas, whose fur was used as lining for pilots' jackets), disinfecting room, and camp brothel, which, according to Franz Goldschmitt *(Zeugen des Abendlandes)*, was disdainfully ignored by ninety-five percent of the prisoners and therefore soon disappeared.

North of Barracks 30 was the administration building for the gardens, called "the plantation" by the prisoners. The plantation, with about sixty buildings, mills, yards, drying plants, market sheds, and offices, spread out right from the fenced-in camp, therefore outside the real area of the prisoners. Between the farm buildings and the barracks was the large parade ground. The prisoners had to assemble there twice a day. Sometimes they were physically punished there, especially those who had failed in an escape attempt. From there, the prisoners marched in work groups and with a "song on their lips" to their places of labor. Here they returned "singing and happy." Occasionally the camp orchestra played stirring marches. It was here that the infamous selections of naked prisoners for the so-called "cripples' transport" (to the gas chambers in Hartheim near Linz) took place. Here sick prisoners were assigned to the infirmary. Here the prisoners had to celebrate Hitler's victories during the first years of the war. Here they could occasionally even play sports. "In the camp's terrible years, it was the custom that prisoners who had died before the evening roll-call or during the night had to be carried (as corpses) to the parade ground. They were laid on the ground behind the last row of prisoners of their barracks and counted along with the others. Only after roll-call was it allowed to carry them to the morgue. . . . Prisoners who were condemned to be whipped received twenty-five double lashes. The whole camp had to watch and hear the cries of pain" (H. Carls, *Dachau*).

The approximately 300-meter-long and 30-meter-wide camp street, which was lined with poplar trees, led to the parade ground. Edmond Michelet, a French general and later minister of justice, called the street ironically "Liberty Street." The two poplars standing in front of each barracks were called "blood poplars" by the prisoners because many prisoners died at forced labor when the camp was erected and especially when the trees were planted.

"On this street, the whole life of the camp unfolded from early in the morning, in free time, at noon, until evening. Friends and acquaintances met here to talk. Experiences were exchanged and new friendships made here. In 1942, the street was populated only by Germans, Poles and Czechs. . . . This changed in 1943. Russians, Frenchmen, Belgians, Yugoslavs, Italians, Danes, Norwegians, Hungarians, Spaniards, Ukrainians, Slovenians, Croats, Greeks, Armenians, Romanians, Serbs, and Swiss came. The street resembled the main street of a great world exposition. The German language disappeared more and more. There was a confusion of languages, among which Russian predominated at first, and then French. Discussing politics was strictly forbidden" (H. Carls, ibid.).

Camp Life behind Barbed Wire

Every barracks was just one hundred meters long and nineteen meters wide. It had four lounges and four dormitories, each unit planned for about fifty prisoners. During the war, they were usually hopelessly overcrowded. The toilets and washrooms were between the units, that is, two units had to share toilet and washroom facilities. The toilets had eight bowls and eight urinals. Since there was often a shortage of water, the toilets and urinals could be flushed only early in the morning and late at night.

In the washrooms, there were six large containers along the wall for washing and two larger basins in the middle of the room. Sixteen water jets entered into the basins from the ceiling. The prisoners, bare from the waist up, washed at these six containers and two basins every morning.

The rest rooms were, according to Franz Goldschmitt, "exemplary, practical, and scrupulously clean."

There were tables and stools in the lounges. "Here the prisoners passed their free time reading, writing, mending, playing, and catching lice. Along the windows, there were shoe racks and, along the two walls without windows, small closets (called lockers) with room for mess gear, towel, napkin, and so forth" (Goldschmitt).

In the dormitories stood the beds: wooden bunks three on top of each other, with straw mattresses. The floor of both rooms, the dormitory and the lounge, had always to be polished. One was allowed to walk on them only in sandals, house shoes, or socks. Franz Goldschmitt writes: "You took off your cleaned shoes at the door, carried them barefoot to your shoe rack, and there exchanged them for slippers. You did this annoying operation about twenty times a day."

Meals were served in two shifts. "We stood one behind another with a bowl in our hand and pushed slowly to the trough [large kettle]. In the process, some food was spilled, poured over people's clothes. There were incidents, name calling, scuffles" (Goldschmitt). In good weather, many of the prisoners ate out on the camp street or in the wash rooms. Almost always, eating went very fast. In five minutes, most had eaten, washed their dishes, and put them away.

Besides the hard forced labor, the carrying of mess kettles, snow shoveling in winter, and work in the gravel pit, the prisoners hated most of all bed making. Almost all of the survivors describe this torture. The straw sack, when smoothed out, had to fit exactly into the square bed frame. Smoothing out the sack was a problem. Woe to you if folds or dips were discovered! Much sweat was poured out on this work. The stiff seaweed or hay in the sacks easily crumbled. The linen sheet had to be pulled tight over the whole straw sack and the grey blanket folded in such a way "that the two blue-white stripes on the edge were still just visible. You carefully rolled it over the bed exactly twenty centimeters from the end of the bed (absolutely not nineteen centimeters!) and pulled it up to the pillow. Here it had to lie in steps upon the pillow" (Goldschmitt).

Later, about the spring of 1943, the linen sheets began to disappear. Bed making was no longer taken so seriously. Before that, it had belonged "to one of the worst prison tortures" (Goldschmitt).

The camp was run and often terrorized by about one hundred and fifty *kapos* (work leaders) and the same number of sub-*kapos*. In addition, there was a barracks elder, four unit elders, "and a lot of other lazy scum who liked to act important" (Goldschmitt). We will have many a frightful deed of these prisoners in leading positions to report on later. Many of them were criminals.

Each barracks also had a barber. No prisoner was allowed to shave himself. Most likely, the SS were afraid that a prisoner might cut his own throat in desperation. Twice a month the prisoners' heads were shaved and twice a week their faces. Their whole bodies were shaved each time a louse was found on them. The heads of the Russians and the Italians were sometimes not completely shaved, but a four-centimeter-wide band was left from their foreheads to the back of their necks. The other prisoners mockingly called this strip the "Russian street" or "expressway."

After the roll call every day, the chief reported the number present to the work office. The work office passed the information on to the kitchen.

Those who were not assigned to work had to stay in the barracks during the day and were often frightfully tormented. They were also given nothing to eat and trembled at the sudden command: "All those not assigned to work assemble on the parade ground!" They often had to stand then for hours on the parade ground or in the bathroom; they were searched, divided up, and sometimes sent to other (annihilation) camps. The "invalid transports" sent to Hartheim near Linz, Austria, from 1942 to 1944 were meant for the gas chambers there; they are given as 3,166 in number. For the gas chamber in Dachau did not work from the very beginning; probably it was due to sabotage, even, they say, by a high SS man.

It was different with the crematorium. The first, smaller one was from the year 1940. As a result of Hitler's planned mass executions, a larger one was quickly built in 1942. It was called "Barracks X." Its gas chamber, disguised as a shower room, was never put into operation. Many Polish clergy had to work on the construction of the large crematorium as bricklayers. Since there were many more bodies than the four ovens could reduce to ashes, especially during the starvation year of 1942, the half-burned bones were brought to the bone mill, ground up, and sold to the surrounding farmers as fertilizer.

Bowing to Superiors, Walking on Inferiors

As part of the description of the total concentration camp, the following places must be mentioned:

—the canteen, where the prisoners could sometimes buy extras; from the beginning of 1942 they could do so with cash (each prisoner was allowed to have twenty marks) and later with coupons; here they could buy, among other things, beet jam, oatmeal cookies, cucumbers, clams, snails, and sometimes even cigarettes—all at exorbitant prices;

—the museum with medicines, photos, and models, even of malformed prisoners who had been sent to their death in invalid

transports, or skulls, bones, etc., of unusual size; the camp records office, where there was a record of all the prisoners of the
main camp and the many Dachau branch camps, each one neatly
inscribed on a file card; the camp scribe, a prisoner, together with
the barracks scribes, had to make a report each day;
—the library, which was much used; most of the books had been
taken from prisoners at their arrival in the camp;
—the infirmary (the barracks for the sick), where the sick prisoners were put; the orderlies were prisoners, with an infirmary
chief in command. "A sadistically inclined infirmary chief got
rid of sick prisoners without knowledge of the SS doctor in
charge by means of injections as well as personally invented
tortures." (J. Neuhäusler, *Wie war das im KZ Dachau?*)

Although an SS man was in charge of each barracks (during the
war years he had several barracks), the real "leaders" were the barracks and unit elders as well as the barracks scribes—all prisoners.
Everything depended on them, including how the camp atmosphere
worked itself out in the barracks units.

"All of the administration of the barracks depended on the barracks
scribe," wrote Neuhäusler. "This included reports and lists on the inhabitants and the food, the distribution of mail, etc. The barracks
scribe was the subordinate of the director of the camp records office,
from whom he received all his commands and orders. The prison officials were treated the same as the other prisoners. The SS regarded
them as nothing else but creatures who were not allowed to think for
themselves. For the slightest offense they were given a box on the ears
right on the spot. . . . The prisoners who worked in the prison records office and carried out the job of barracks scribes were people
eighty percent of whom tried to save the prisoners in every possible
situation and procured them relief whenever they could. They did this
without paying attention to nationality, political leaning, etc. In acting
so, they often came into conflict even with the SS directors and the
barracks and camp elders. As time went on, the different camp officials gained so much influence due to the difficult situation on the front
lines that they could save hundreds of prisoners" (ibid.).

Of course, it must be also said that there were among the chiefs
some sadists and torturers who bowed to their superiors and kicked
their subordinates. Neuhäusler says that the camp became "more

human" under Camp Commander Weiß. He introduced helpful changes and forbade the arbitrary beating of prisoners by the *kapos*.

The basic attitude of the SS men was learned "on the spot" in Dachau: the concentration camp was a good place for the "internship" of the young SS leaders. "They had to guard people who thought differently than themselves, perhaps had to beat them, maybe even kill them, in order to win their SS diploma. It was daily drilled into them that the inhabitants of the concentration camp were enemies of the state, Jews, traitors; in short, worthless lives" (M. von der Grün, *Wie war das eigentlich?*).

Practically all the SS were trained in Dachau. Adolf Eichmann was lieutenant platoon commander here (1934); here Rudolf Höss, the infamous camp commander of Auschwitz, "trained" as barracks leader and the one in charge of reports (1934–38). The brutality and hardheartedness of these men schooled in Dachau shows through in the autobiographical notes of Rudolf Höss, written during his own imprisonment in Krakow from 1946 to 1947: "The Jews who were marked for annihilation [in the Auschwitz concentration camp—ed.] were led to the crematorium as quietly as possible, men and women separate. They were told in their own language by the prisoners of the special squad employed there that they had come there only to bathe and be deloused, that they should fold their clothes neatly and above all remember where they laid them so that they could find them quickly after the delousing. . . . After undressing, they went into the gas chambers which, equipped with water pipes and showers, looked totally like bathing rooms. . . . An SS man remained with the prisoners in the chamber until the last minute. The door was then quickly screwed shut, and containers of gas standing ready were thrown into openings in the roof of the chamber through air passages to the floor. One could see through the observation holes that those standing next to the air passages immediately fell over dead. It can be said that one third of the people were dead immediately. The others began to stagger, shout, and fight for air. The shouting however soon became a death-rattle, and in a few minutes all lay dead. . . . A special squad now removed gold teeth and cut off the women's hair. From here the bodies were brought up by elevator to the ovens, which had in the meantime been heated."

Höss continues: "I observed that women who suspected or knew what was coming, with the fear of death in their eyes, still found the strength to joke with their children and to speak kindly to them. Once a woman, in going by, walked up very close to me and whispered to me as she pointed to her four children, 'How can you kill these beautiful, lovely children? Don't you have any heart in your body?'—An old man once said to me in passing, 'Germany will have to pay dearly for these mass murders of Jews.' His eyes glowed with hatred" (*Kommandant in Auschwitz*).

Although the Dachau prisoners were spared this kind of horror because, as we have said, the gas chambers never functioned, they nevertheless knew about the fate of those who were carried off to the annihilation camps, that is, to Hartheim. And prisoners from those camps had come to them. Through them, the prisoners in Dachau were quite well informed about what was going on in Auschwitz, Mauthausen, Flossenbürg, and other concentration camps. Of course, it is true here what Martin Walser once said: "Only the prisoners knew what Auschwitz was. No one else!" That is true, by the way, of every concentration camp, including Dachau. For that reason, eye witnesses and reports of former prisoners of Dachau will be quoted often in this book.

Plan for Systematic Annihilation at Hitler's Command

"Destruction of vermin" is what the Nazis called the millions of murders of Jews, Gypsies, Russians, Poles, invalids, "anti-social people," and clergy. Hitler gave the first written order for the destruction of the sick on precisely the first day of the Second World War. By this order of the Führer on September 1, 1939, about 100,000 Germans, "useless eaters," were officially killed in the next two years. They were mostly patients of convalescent and extended care homes, many of them children. (The figures quoted here are based on Sebastian Haffner's book, *Anmerkungen zu Hitler*. Most of the following figures also come from this documented work.)

The rooting out of "unworthy life" ran into strong criticism, especially from the churches, so Hitler suspended it in 1941. The campaign of the destruction of the Gypsies also began in September 1939. "Estimations of those murdered go as high as 500,000. In any case, of the approximately 25,000 Gypsies who lived in Germany in 1939 only about 5,000 were alive in 1945" (Haffner).

In October 1939, after the "victorious Polish campaign," Hitler ordered the extirpation of the Polish intelligentsia. That included all of those who belonged to the educated classes: priests, teachers, professors, journalists, business men. That any at all of the interned Polish clergy survived at all was due partly to the fact that in 1940–41 they were "transferred" to Dachau, probably at the repeated pressing of Pope Pius XII, who again and again referred to the concordat between the Third Reich and the Vatican and demanded that at least the clergy receive some small mitigations.

A commemorative article of May 1940 by Heinrich Himmler shows how very much the Nazis considered the people of the "Eastern Regions" especially as "second class citizens": "For the non-German people of the East, there cannot be any schools higher than the fourth grade of elementary school. The goal of these elementary schools must be only to teach simple arithmetic up to at most 500, the ability to write one's name, and that it is a divine law to be obedient to the Germans, honest, industrious and well-behaved" (Haffner).

From the middle of 1941 on, "Hitler's most extensive mass murder" of the Jews of Poland, Russia, Germany, and finally of all the occupied areas was in operation. It was a systematic "destruction of the Jewish race in Europe" (Hitler). The number of murdered Jews reached "according to the lowest estimations over four million and according to the highest almost six million" (Haffner).

Dr. Hans Frank, Hitler's former governor in Poland, wrote in his sketches, *In Face of the Gallows*, that Hitler was one of the worst and cruelest criminals of human history: "Around his name, it reeks of millions of corpses, ruins, hunger, decline, rot, and cruelty. He was the greatest dynamic human cause of destruction which humanity has had to put up with until now."

Haffner compares Hitler's destructive vanity with that of a horse breeder: "At the end, Hitler acted like a hot-tempered, disappointed owner of a race horse stable who had his best horse beaten to death because it was not able to win the Derby."

Torments and Ill Treatment

Even if, as we have said, the Dachau concentration camp was not an "annihilation camp" in the strict sense, the attitude of the SS there was generally that of executioners. Although it was not a "death factory," killing nevertheless went on continually—through work, deprivation, hunger, sickness, arbitrary murder, shootings, pseudo-scientific experiments of the SS doctors, and many other torments.

For example, on Good Friday 1940, sixty clergymen had to go on the "tree" for an hour. Their hands were tied behind their backs and fastened to a chain. They were then "hung up" by these chains until their feet no longer touched the ground. Jean Bernard writes: "This punishment, which was inflicted on sixty clergymen just on Good Friday, was so terrible that the next year we looked forward to Good Friday with trembling. We were threatened with it for months. It was a bad Lent. We hardly dared to breathe, in order not to give them an excuse for using it. Several died during the torture. Many came away with a crippled hand" (*Pfarrerblock 25487*).

There was also the day when an SS man gave the command: "All clerical pigs get under the tables immediately! With the tables on your head, stand up, kneel down, stand up, and so forth. So it went back and forth until the unfortunate ones were totally exhausted. Then came a new order: Immediately get on top of the lockers! Sit down! Now together sing 'O Sacred Head Surrounded'" (Goldsch-mitt, ibid.).

The Austrian parish priest Siegfried Würl, as several former concentration camp priests reported, once had to lie for twenty minutes in ice cold snow up to his neck at the command of an SS man. In the meantime, an SS man stood on his back. Another time, the same priest, who had been sent to the concentration camp in Sachsenhausen in November 1939 and brought to Dachau in December 1940, had to stand for an hour in the camp street, "look up uninterruptedly at the sun, wave to it, and continually shout: 'Come, dear sun, come and heal my nose!'" (Goldschmitt).

The confinement, being watched continually with machine guns, the unremitting fear ("You will never get out of here!"), the electrified barbed wire, the walls, the moat fed by the Amper River, the watch towers, the death strip—all that produced an anxiety which ate its way deeper and deeper into the soul.

One time, a Catholic priest ran into the electric wire; he was from the infirmary, where he had been lying with a high fever. He was immediately spotted by the guard and ordered to halt. The priest, in his delirium, did not pay any attention to the warning shot either, but pointed to his heart and cried out: "Shoot here!" At the moment that he grasped the wire, the guard shot him. He was dead on the spot.

It was no less depressing to the prisoners that they were continually surrounded by spies and denouncers "who reported every sharp or presumed sharp word to the party or the Gestapo" (Neuhäusler).

Nevertheless, every now and then there were individual prisoners who reacted, who showed the courage to stand up even to the SS eyeball to eyeball. Individual incidents will be reported later. Here we bring only one small episode described by Johann Nuehäusler (*Saat des Bösen*, Mainz, 1964). An SS storm trooper platoon leader had cursed and sworn against God, Christ, and His church in an obscene manner in front of hundreds of clergymen. When he finally paused, the clear and distinct voice of the Luxemburg pastor Johann Brachmond resounded from the ranks of the clergymen: "And still the gates of hell will not overcome it." Fear gripped the other clergymen. They feared for the life of the courageous confessor and dreaded the worst for themselves. But the SS man was so taken aback that he turned around and left without saying a word. Brachmond later, on October 17, 1941, suffered a miserable death in the Dachau concentration camp.

After these general "impressions" of the Dachau concentration camp, we want to turn to Father Engelmar Unzeitig, who came to Dachau in 1941 at the age of thirty and died there four years later of typhus. In order to understand his martyrdom in all its profundity and consequences, we must get to know his life, look back at his origins, his education, and his studies and try to grasp his personal fears and difficulties. Only then will it become clear to us how great a confessor and martyr the quiet and modest Mariannhill Missionary was. His future matured in his past.

2

CHILDHOOD AND YOUTH

Father Engelmar Unzeitig came from the Schönhengst District, an island of Germans north of Brno in Czechoslovakia. He was born there on March 1, 1911, in Greifendorf (today Hradec n. Svitavy), baptized three days later (March 4), and given the name of Hubert. The family name Unzeitig(er) was very common in the Schönhengst District. Its first written record is from the year 1535, where it appears as "Unczayt" or "Unczaytyk." In Middle High German it was written "Unzitec." The name means "unfitting, not happening at the right time."

Hubert's parents were simple people. They ran a modest farm in Greifendorf. His mother, Maria Unzeitig (née Kohl), was from Oberheinzendorf in the Schönhengst District and his father, Johann Unzeitig, came from a farm family in Pohler. They had six children (four girls and two boys).

An autobiography, written by Hubert when he was seventeen, describes very beautifully the simple atmosphere of his home and the village character of his birth place.

"I was born in Greifendorf (in the wonderful Schönhengst District) on March 1, 1911. My parents were simple, upright farmers who migrated to Greifendorf from the surrounding area. They acquired a small farm there, which my mother still [1928—ed.] owns. I passed my childhood in the beloved home of my parents with my four sisters. (Death took my only brother in his first year of life.) I also lived there during my school years. My parents lived there for nine happy years until the bloody World War with its serious consequences broke out in 1914. My father was among the first ones who had to move out against the Russian enemy. He was soon captured and transported far into the Russian empire to Simbirsk on the Volga, where he soon got sick and, on January 14, 1916, died of typhus. When the sad news was brought to us, my mother was beside herself because we children were all still small and in school, which meant that my mother would have to continue farming with only hired help. But by and by, times improved because we finished school one after another. This year my youngest sister was fourteen, so we also shared the work and worry with my mother" (GA).

As Christian parents, Maria and Johann Unzeitig were concerned with raising Hubert, as well as his sisters, religiously from the earliest age. They knew that religion does not come to children by itself, but they must encounter it in the family. They therefore carried out their responsibility as Christian parents with decision and conviction.

After the loss of her husband, the mother had to take in hand the religious upbringing of her children alone. She did it with the greatest naturalness and with much love and patience. On May 16, 1920, at the age of nine, Hubert received his First Communion. On September 26, 1921, he was confirmed by Bishop Dr. Karl Wisnar in the parish church of Zwittau.

Hubert's sister Maria-Huberta recalls: "Our home was very religious. Mother prayed much. On Sunday mornings, we all went to Mass, on Sunday afternoons to Benediction. Hubert always liked to go along. We girls (his sisters) considered him a pious boy. . . . As children, we went to daily Mass. The school was next door to the church. Sometimes we also went to the Redemptorist church at Vierzighuben. That is on the way to Zwittau, about a half hour on foot. Our church was always full. The people of Greifendorf were good Catholics."

The love of God, therefore, was planted in Hubert's heart when he was still young. He built on that foundation. With time, he developed a deeply religious attitude and exhibited a praiseworthy behavior toward the world around him. In grade school, too, which he attended from September 16, 1917, to June 27, 1925 (a time of war and terrible hunger), he was conspicuous for his great piety, blameless conduct, and enormous diligence.

His results in school were also quite exemplary. His grades on his graduating grade school report card were: conduct "praiseworthy";

application "persevering." He received a "very good" in all other subjects, that is, in religion, social studies, reading, grammar, composition, geography, history, science, arithmetic, drawing, writing, singing, manual labor, gymnastics, Czech, and neatness. An all-A student!

High German was practiced in school, but the Schönhengst dialect, which has many similarities to the Franconian dialect, was used at home.

After grade school, Hubert worked for August Janka, a farmer in Vresice (parish of Kretin, Diocese of Brünn), as a farmhand to improve his Czech somewhat. He was only fourteen or fifteen years old, but he had to do just about all of the work of a farmhand except carry very heavy loads.

Hubert remained one year to the day in Vresice, from July 9, 1925, to July 9, 1926. Then he returned to Greifendorf and helped his mother and sisters on their own farm.

A few memories of Hubert's sister Maria-Huberta, loosely strung together, can help us to get a little better acquainted with the now fifteen-year-old young man. "Hubert did not have any friends or girl friends; he had to work hard on the farm. But he often buried himself in books. Reading was his hobby from when he was young. He borrowed books from the pastor and from the Catholic club house. . . . When he came back from the Czechs [his one year service in Vresice—ed.], mother had bought him a bicycle. With it, he took a look at the surrounding areas on Sundays. Otherwise, however, he was always sitting with his books. At home, we often played cards and other games. Then we girls also played. . . . Our mother spoke Czech very well. On Sunday afternoons, we often went to Pohler, on foot, to visit grandmother. Hubert always went along; only the two youngest had to stay home. Grandmother often read to us out of the Mariannhill magazine. It was called *Vergissmeinnicht* at that time and was sent to us through Austria. At that time, too, my brother's later vocation was most likely awakened" (GA).

In fact, at this time, Hubert's wish to be a priest and missionary matured. He spoke to his mother about it (she gave her consent, but with a heavy heart, because he was the only male to take over the farm) and consulted with a priest at the Monastery of Vierzighuben. Then he wrote to the Mariannhill Missionaries in Reimlingen, Ries, and asked for admission.

Hubert Unzeitig wrote about his decision to become a priest and missionary: "I felt impelled to join the service of Christ for the saving of souls. Having been made aware of the missions by the Mariannhill magazines and calendars, I decided to dedicate my life to the conversion of the pagans. In the beginning, people tried to dissuade me and pointed out the shortage of priests at home. Enquiries were made here and there, but to my great surprise and joy I received unfavorable answers everywhere. Above all, I was too old (seventeen) for the ordinary course of studies. Nevertheless, the seminary in Reimlingen promised to remove all difficulties" (GA).

So it turned out. Hubert Unzeitig received his admission papers from the missionary seminary in Reimlingen by mail.

Father Gustav Schneider (born in Greifendorf), who was driven from his Czechoslovakian home in 1946, remembers those times: "I was already in my studies when Hubert was still working at home on the farm. I lived in Mitteldorf, he in Oberdorf near the parish border. He was older than I. Only after he began his studies and came more often to church even on week days, did we have somewhat closer contact. He was an introvert and serious by nature. He suffered much, I believe, because, in following his goal, he had to leave most of the work at home to his sisters. His very pious mother, especially, saw in him, her only male child, the future heir of the farm. When he did not give in at all, she went to the Redemptorist monastery in Vierzighub to get advice. After the priest had interviewed our Hubert alone and his mother came in, she received the answer: 'Let him study. God is calling here.' It was a great sacrifice, but she said, 'Yes.' Other still more difficult 'yeses' would follow. . . . Besides to God, Hubert owed his vocation, I believe, to his deeply religious home, especially to his mother. Mariannhill mission magazines, which were kept in his home, most likely gave the direction to his vocation. He wanted, you see, to be a missionary and to bring the Good News to people who did not yet know anything about Jesus" (letter to the editor, December 1980).

3

SECONDARY SCHOOL AND UNIVERSITY

On April 18, 1928, Hubert entered the Mariannhill seminary for late vocations in Reimlingen, Ries. There were approximately sixty students there who had come to get their secondary school diploma and then become priests and missionaries. Reimlingen lies about three kilometers south of Nördlingen, about equally distant from Stuttgart, Nürnberg, and Augsburg.

Hubert did not come to Reimlingen alone. Another late vocation was with him: Ansbert Karl Bieberle from Krönau near Moravian Trübau, about seventeen kilometers from Greifendorf. After having been admitted to Reimlingen independently of one another, they got to know each other in Greifendorf. Ansbert was twelve years older than Hubert.

Now the "freshmen" had to hit the books for six years. Hubert did so with great commitment and much success. His secondary school report cards, which are kept in the Mariannhill archives in Rome, show that he was a very talented and exceptionally diligent student.

Even more revealing than his grades, which were all A's and B's, were the remarks of his teachers on the report cards. For example, on his report card of 1931–1932 it is written: "Very intelligent and energetic, very gifted." In 1933–34: "Open, upright look which inspires trust. Very gifted; good in gymnastics. Very intelligent, deep thinker, mature, hungry for knowledge (studies the conversational lexicon!), skilled in literary description. Outstanding character, absolutely dependable and loyal even in little things, enormously diligent, a (genuine) personality. Exceptionally fit for university studies. In spite of his great intelligence, very modest and restrained, and therefore well fit for religious community. Leadership qualities" (GA).

The director of the seminary for late vocations at that time, Father Ludwig Tremel, was also full of praise for Hubert Unzeitig. In an extra report card of 1934 he wrote: "A healthy, talented, very motivated, very conscientious, and very dependable student. Deeply pious, but somewhat timid. Enjoys the respect of teachers and students" (GA).

In April 1934—Hitler had been in power more than a year— Hubert graduated from the congregation's secondary school. Since he had decided to join the Mariannhill Mission Congregation, he began a one-year novitiate in St. Paul near Arcen, Holland. The investiture was on April 30, 1934.

The year passed very quickly with work, prayer, and study. Hubert Unzeitig had received a new name at his clothing: Frater (later Father) Engelmar. From then on he would be called by that religious name. On May 1, 1935, the novice who was called by his superiors and confreres "very friendly, helpful, and zealous" made his first profession.

After the novitiate, Frater Engelmar and his classmates moved to Mariannhill's Pius Seminary in Würzburg. There he studied theology and philosophy for five years. The gifted and diligent student used every free minute for reading, learned many modern languages besides his regular studies—French, English, Italian, Czech, and Russian—and read through whole encyclopedias. On May 1, 1938, he made his final profession.

And so it went. On February 19, 1939, Frater Engelmar was ordained subdeacon. Three weeks later on March 5, he was ordained deacon. Finally on August 6 of the same year, he was ordained priest in the Mariannhill Sacred Heart Church in Würzburg. The new priest celebrated his First Mass in his home village of Greifendorf on August 15, 1939, the Feast of the Assumption.

While Father Engelmar was still at home, the Second World War broke out. On September 1, 1939, Hitler had German soldiers cross the Polish border without a formal declaration of war. Father Engelmar returned to Würzburg and for one year prepared for his pastoral exam, which gave him the authority to exercise all the priestly functions.

At the end of his pastoral year (summer of 1940), Father Engelmar was assigned to the recently founded Mariannhill province of Austria with headquarters in Riedegg, Upper Austria. Certainly he would have liked to go home to visit his mother and sisters once again, but the Second World War had begun in earnest. He would never see Greifendorf again.

4

ARREST IN GLÖCKELBERG

There were about thirty French prisoners of war in Riedegg Castle near Gallneukirchen (Diocese of Linz) in the middle of 1940. The prisoners were employed by the farmers nearby to help with the harvest. The Mariannhill Missionaries also received four prisoners for their farm.

Father Engelmar, who had come to help out in the parishes, was given the assignment to care for these thirty men. His outstanding knowledge of French served him well here. Although it was strictly forbidden, every Sunday he celebrated Mass for the prisoners, who were all Catholics, and gave a short sermon in French. He took care of the French prisoners of war in other ways, too, with great pastoral zeal.

In late summer of 1940, the Bishop of Linz asked the Mariannhill Missionaries to supply him, as far as possible, with pastors for the various parishes in the Bohemian Woods. They agreed to it. Father Engelmar was among those priests who immediately declared their willingness to help.

Then Father Engelmar was sent to Glöckelberg, not far from the Austrian border, only about twenty-five kilometers from Freistadt, near Oberplan, the home of the famous poet Adalbert Stifter (1805–1868). Here on October 1, 1940, he began his first pastoral assignment as parish administrator. His sister Maria-Huberta was with him as his housekeeper.

According to the description of one of his confreres, Father Engelmar lived "like a hermit" in the Glöckelberg rectory. He hardly had enough firewood and only the most necessary furniture; he was short of everything. In addition, the winter of 1940–41 was very severe; there was much snow.

In spite of the frugal living conditions and the severe winter, Father Engelmar took the pastoral task assigned to him very seriously. He made many house visits in order to get to know his community, often cheered up old and sick people by coming, and prepared himself well for his Sunday sermons and his religion classes in the school.

It was in the school that the Mariannhill Father first got into trouble with members of the Hitler Youth organization. The clear answers which Father Engelmar gave to the tricky questions of the Hitler Youth and his consistent announcement of the Gospel and the teaching of Christ went too far for some of the Nazi spies. Father Engelmar was reported and arrested on April 21, 1941. According to the collection *Austrian Priests in Prisons and Concentration Camps of the Nazi Regime* by Johann Mittendorfer, Father Engelmar was accused of "insidious expressions" in sermons and instructions and "defense of the Jews."

Father Engelmar's sister Maria-Huberta describes his arrest by the Gestapo: "On April 21, 1941, my brother was arrested by two Gestapo in the rectory in Glöckelberg. Once before he had been summoned. Evidently he was undesirable or simply too pious for the Nazis. On that day—it was a Monday—I was visiting an old woman parishioner in the village; from her house I could see very well across to the rectory. Suddenly I noticed a car there and this frightened me a little. Shortly afterward my brother appeared and said: 'Look, the Gestapo is here! Come along quickly!' The two men were already looking through everything in the parish office. They paged through my brother's sermon notes and took some of them along. Hubert was deathly pale as he got his small suitcase in order to pack a few things. I was not even able to make him something to eat. I would have liked to cook something for him. But everything went very fast. . . . On the next day, I closed the rectory and went to stay with that old woman whom I knew. Later she moved into the rectory with me so I would not be alone. She had made everything known in the community: that there would be no Mass, nor religious instruction either. Then we said the rosary in church and sang the hymn 'Severe Judge of All Sinners'. . . . The people went home in silence. Many of them wept. Most of the residents of Glöckelberg were deeply moved" (from interviews and letters, GA).

On the very day of his arrest, Father Engelmar was brought to prison in Linz on the Danube. Many of his confreres were convinced that an error had been made. He himself also believed that there was a mistake, as he expressed in a letter of April 23, 1941, to his sister. He hoped to be released soon from prison: "Dear sister, you don't need to worry too much about me, since I did not commit any crime. It must be a misunderstanding. They tell me it will take about twenty days" (GA).

But Father Engelmar's hopes were not fulfilled. The Nazi machinery had become so overpowering that there was hardly any chance for even "small sinners" to be freed. The war was going on. The attack on Russia ("after a victorious French campaign") would follow in a few weeks. Hitler and his likes were at the height of their power. In addition to the Jews (who from January 9, 1941, on were forced to wear the Star of David), they had it in especially for the Catholic clergy. Since they were afraid to imprison bishops, they harassed the lower clergy all the more brutally. "We must bring it about that only imbeciles will be preaching and only little old ladies will be listening to them. The healthy youth is on our side," Hitler said in 1941. And he continued: "The greatest damage for the people are our pastors of both denominations. The moment will come when I will settle accounts with them without much ceremony. I will not be tripped up by legal hairsplitting then. Expediency alone will be decisive. . . . While in the Party, I never cared to what denomination those around me belonged. When I am buried, I would not like to have a clergyman within ten kilometers. If such a one could help me, I would doubt Providence. I act as I see and understand. . . . I am here because of a higher Power" (H. Picker, *Hitlers Tischgespräche*).

After six weeks of fearful waiting in the Linz prison, the order came for Father Engelmar from Berlin: Dachau. With that began a completely new and very painful chapter of his young priestly life.

5

IN THE DACHAU HELL

"Arrived here in Dachau on June 3. Am healthy." With these brief words, Father Engelmar began his first letter written in the Dachau concentration camp. The recipient was his sister Maria-Huberta, who for the time being still lived in Glöckelberg, then moved back to Greifendorf, and, after the death of their mother (1943), went to live with her sister in Pohler, the birthplace of their father.

The letters which Father Engelmar wrote from Dachau will be discussed extensively in the following pages. First, however, as a continuation of Chapter 1, something should be said about admission to the concentration camp, about the "entry camp," as the admissions barracks was called by the prisoners, and about the daily schedule inside the electric barbed wire fence.

As they came to Dachau, it was clear to most of the prisoners that there was no hope for a quick release, if any release at all. Chained together, they could expect anything. Of course, they had no idea what awaited them. Otherwise they could not have survived the anxiety and fear. No one who had not been in a concentration camp before could know what went on there.

Father Engelmar was just as poorly informed as the thousands of others who came to Dachau that year. Once they came to the Dachau railroad station, the prisoners usually had to wait first of all. They had to wait, stand around, often for hours, under the burning sun or in freezing cold, in rain, snow, and stormy weather. They were laughed at by the SS who passed by.

Through the gateway of the Jourhaus (guard building at the entrance to the concentration camp), the prisoners came to the "waiting room." Here they had to strip and give up all their belongings. From now on, they had only prisoners' clothes. On a small piece of paper, each new arrival was given a number, which from now on he always had to wear.

Then the prisoners were shaved all over their bodies. Their hair was cut to a half millimeter length. Everything had to be done quickly. The hair cutting and shaving (including the private parts) was sometimes a torture because dull hair clippers were often used. It was always degrading. Those who had been shorn were painted all over with a strong disinfectant which smelled and burned the skin. Then it was washed off in the shower. The showers were either ice cold or steaming hot, depending on the mood of the SS man who operated them.

The prison uniforms were too small or too large for most of the prisoners. The SS joked about this. Every now and then, one of them would shout, when a prisoner's cap was too small: "In four weeks, everything will fit, including this cap!" In addition, each one received only a pair of wooden shoes or cloth shoes with wood soles, a metal bowl, silverware, and a drinking mug. If he was lucky, he also received socks and underwear.

The psychological strain, partly caused by the outward humiliation, the continual shouting of the SS, the wearing of a number, and the loss of all rights, was the hardest thing for a prisoner to bear at the beginning of his time in the concentration camp. He was in fact now only a number. Father Engelmar's number, which he now had to wear on all his clothing, was 26 147. Whenever he met an SS man, he had to stand at attention and, with cap in hand, greet him: "Prisoner 26 147 Unzeitig Hubert reports most obediently for duty!" (or: "asks for permission to enter!")

Outcasts of the Human Race

Immediately on the first day, right after arriving in the camp, every prisoner had to fill out a long questionnaire. Here it is in the Nazi formulation, slightly condensed and shortened:

I. Family name, first name, type of imprisonment, prisoner number, barracks, barracks unit, arrival date, transferred from, retransferred from, released to. . . .

II. Profession

III. Date of birth, place of birth, address

IV. Religion

V. Single/married/widowed/divorced; wife, children, children's ages, children's occupations

VI. Size, weight, color of hair, color of eyes, body shape

VII. Tattoos, on which parts of the body

VIII. Father's age, mother's age, in case of death give cause of death and age at the time of death

IX. Physical or psychological sicknesses of mother or father: TB, blindness, deafness, malformation, alcoholism, nervous condition, time in mental hospital

X. Have there been any of the sicknesses mentioned in IX in your family? If so, who had them? Exact details. . . .

XI. Have there been suicide attempts in the prisoner's family? By whom? Are there indications of criminal or antisocial tendencies (transgressions against morality, other people's property or acts of violence; begging, vagrancy; crimes under the influence of alcohol? By whom?

XII. What sicknesses has the prisoner himself had, when and where was he treated for them?

XIII. What schools did the prisoner attend, when and where? What were his grades, how often did he fail?

XIV. Did the prisoner attend a school/institution for the retarded? When, where? Name of the school/institution

XV. Was the prisoner ever assigned to child welfare work? When? In what institution?

XVI. Has the prisoner had any previous convictions? What were they? In what court . . . ?

XVII. Has the prisoner been addicted to any drug? Which one? Was he assigned to any withdrawal program? When? What were the results?

XVIII. Is the prisoner a nonsmoker? For how long? Was he formerly a smoker? Until when? Is he a nondrinker? Since when? Was he formerly a drinker? Until when?

Finally the prisoner had to sign the questionnaire. Below was added in small print: "I have been informed that false information or withholding of information is liable to severe penalty."

On the same form, the SS also assessed the external appearance of the prisoner. Among other things they marked the following with an X: Build: strong, thick-set, slim, weakly; Nose: straight, hooked, turned up, large, small; Mouth: thin, thick, protruding lips; Ears: large, small, prominent; Teeth: complete, partly missing, gold teeth; Speech: dialect, stutter, stammer, etc. The whole procedure of the questionnaires, as also the admission procedure, was meant to break down the prisoner's self-respect and dignity.

In addition, every prisoner was exteriorly "branded" by a chevron sewn on his pants and jacket. Political prisoners had a red chevron, criminals a green one, antisocial prisoners a black one, homosexuals a pink one, emigrants a blue one, and the Jehovah's Witnesses a purple one. Sometimes the foreigners also had to wear a letter in their chevron, for example, P for Polish, C for Czech, F for French.

Repeat prisoners, that is, those who had been sent to Dachau for a second time, wore a crossbar to their chevron. Whoever had attempted to escape received a circle (red) with a point in the middle. Prisoners from the Wehrmacht (regular German army) wore a red chevron upside down. Jewish prisoners wore a second, yellow triangle under the usual chevron. It had to be sewn on in such a way that the two corners of the yellow triangle shown out from under the two ends of the upper chevron.

Thus every prisoner was always able to be "ranked" by the SS. Almost all of the clergymen bore red chevrons/triangles; they belonged to the political prisoners. Jean Bernard (ibid.) writes about the way the chevrons were sewn on: "I received two fifteen-centimeter-long pieces of cloth with the number 25 487 printed in black on them and two bright red triangles of about ten centimeters. Sew them on immediately! That is, on the left side of my jacket and on the right side of my pants. Our fellow prisoners help us. All at once one of them has a needle. Another shows us how to get a piece of thread. The seam of my jacket is cut open and a thread is pulled out of the cloth. I am usually not unhandy, but to sew a cloth triangle on a jacket in such a way that neither the triangle nor the jacket is pulled out of shape and that one corner of the triangle points down perfectly so that the opposite side lies nicely parallel to the numbers sewed above it, that made me sweat."

The Lutheran pastor Ernst Wilm writes, in addition: "We were no longer anything but numbers, no longer human beings, just outcasts of humanity. The camp director said as much: 'You have come here because the people's community has rejected you!'" (*Dachau*).

The daily schedule in the camp looked like this:

5:00	(in summer an hour earlier) rising, washing, breakfast, making of beds, room cleaning
6:00	roll call, work time
12:00	dinner
13:00	to 18:30 work time
19:00	roll call (length: up to an hour, often with vexations and tortures)
20:45	return to the barracks
21:00	lights out

In winter, the work time lasted from dawn until dusk.

The rations in the camp were: in the morning 350 grams of bread for the whole day and a half liter of artificial coffee; at noon one liter of turnip or cabbage soup (six days a week; on Sundays noodle soup); in the evening three quarters of a liter of tea, four times a week twenty-five grams of sausage or cheese, and three times a week a liter of soup.

All in all—with the hard work which the prisoners had to do— a starvation diet! Many died in a few months of undernourishment, weakness, hunger edema (dropsy of the connective tissues), and circulatory problems. Other frequent sicknesses were frostbite, carbuncles (abscesses of the hair follicles spread over several areas of the body), phlegmons (pussy infection of cellular tissue), TB, scabies, shingles, and typhus.

"Only the Devil Laughs Here"

The language of the SS was brutal and sometimes sarcastic: "Everyone out! Move! You clergy pigs, now we'll teach you a few things! We'll teach you to run, you pigs, you full stomachs! Everything is too narrow for these fat priests! Everything will fit after a few months" (S. Hess, *Dachau*).

For Monsignor Joseph Albinger, also a former Dachau prisoner, the worst humiliation of his life was the admittance procedure: "From that time on, the guards were continually on the heels of the prisoner. He was suddenly plunged into an international world of suffering. A confusion of languages from many nations pressed upon him. In this hell, even the prisoners became rough and brutal" (SvD 5/66).

The continual shouting from the SS wore the prisoners down. As the pastor Richard Schneider reports, the SS commander of the camp told the newcomers of his attitude in the following way:

"You have stopped being human beings. You have been thrown out of human society. Now you are only numbers. If a number drops out, it can be worn by another. Whoever commits a small offence here will lengthen his stay by months; whoever commits a serious offence will lengthen it by years. Dismissed!" (FDA/1970).

"No one laughs here. The only one who laughs is the devil, and the devil, that's me!" grinning maliciously, SS Platoon Leader Tränkle shouted at the "newcomers" (R. Schnabel, ibid.).

The threats, the terror, the fear, being crowded together, the poor clothing (much too little for the cold time of the year), working long hours in the rain, the continual drilling in military tone—all that worked tremendously on the nerves of the prisoners. A signboard on the roofs of the farm buildings announced in big letters: "There is a way to freedom. Its milestones are: Obedience, honesty, cleanliness, sobriety, diligence, truthfulness, order, and love of the Fatherland." These words grinned down on the prisoners every day as sheer mockery.

Camp life, as Raimund Schnabel (ibid.) rightly saw, mercilessly tore away from the face of the person who had to bear all that every kind of mask which had hidden his "naked self," often for years, from the criticism of his neighbors. "The sheared, naked councillor of commerce, as also the sheared and naked Protestant senior minister next to him in the prison bath of the Dachau concentration camp, both of whom were being painted with evil smelling disinfectant by a professional criminal who was serving time for highway robbery, rape, and break-in, would have experienced only mocking laughter, had he wanted to insist upon his social privileges. If he had character, if he were a real person, he could expect to be accepted in spite of, not because of, his past. . . . Here the straw was separated from the wheat; only what had weight withstood this strong wind. And it became clear that the line of decency of character ran across all classes and nations. Whoever was an exaggerated nationalist was cured in the concentration camp, because the friendly Frenchman was closer to him than, say, the German fellow countryman who denounced him to the SS."

The main objective was to make all prisoners the same. It is easy to understand that the clergy suffered most under this, since they were especially respected in society, yes, even raised above it.

The common toilets, the dented aluminum pots for getting food, the uniformity of the whole camp life ("Whoever had seen a concentration camp living area with sleeping quarters, toilet, wash room, etc., was acquainted with the whole camp," Hess) had a depressing effect on anyone who had not done anything wrong in his life. The prison clothes turned one into a clown. At night, one was not allowed to keep any clothes on in bed, not even in the middle of ice cold winter.

Three dozen prisoners were tortured to death because one prisoner kept his shorts on in bed. Father Sales Hess tells the story. A drunken SS man went through the barracks with several companions, checked the beds, found the "sinner," and began shooting. "When they ran out of ammunition, the barbarians picked up stools and began hitting the prisoners. By the next morning, thirty-seven defenseless people lay dead on their straw mattresses, along with many other lightly and seriously wounded persons" (ibid.).

"Don't Put Any Nonsense in Your Head"

Father Hermann Dümig, who came to Dachau only one day after Father Engelmar and knew him well through all the years until his death, describes the brutal treatment of the newcomers by the SS in an eighty-page manuscript.

> We had hardly arrived in the camp when the review of our personal records began. Two clergymen were among the fifty-five arrivals. . . . In most cases, the camp commander Zill accompanied his paging through the documents with biting sarcasm. He delivered kicks and slaps left and right, although some missed their mark because of the quick ducks of the prisoners. The filthy language and vile insinuations which were spoken here cannot be repeated. The worst thing that I ever heard in my life was a blasphemous attack on the Incarnation

of Christ through Mary. One of the highest SS men shouted in a rage: "We will bring the pastor of Dachau and Bishop Galen of Münster here yet and gag their impudent mouths! These clergy pigs must disappear from the face of the earth!"

After the humiliating review of personal papers, came the infamous picture taking for the criminal album of the SS justice department. When the picture-taking was over, the "criminal" sprang up as he was stuck in the seat by a metal point, much to the malicious pleasure of the SS men. What was especially humiliating was the next procedure. The prisoners were driven through the shower under continual shouting and cursing. . . . Then everyone received a shirt, a zebra-striped denim suit, and a pair of wooden clogs without socks. The top of the clogs was made of woven wood fiber, which rubbed open the skin after a few steps. Clumsily and sometimes falling down like little children while they did so, the "newcomers" walked across the stony parade ground, which was built for 10,000 men but had to hold 32,000 prisoners toward the end of the war, to the admissions barracks No. 9, whose barracks elder was a man by the name of Gutmann, a communist, and an editor by profession. He spoke to the newly admitted in the following way: "Friends, you have not come to a convalescent home. You have to work here. No one can loaf. Life is tough. The punishments are barbarian. Whoever steals bread will be beaten to death. There is no God in the camp; no one has ever seen him. Don't put any nonsense in your head, as if you will soon be released. The normal way to freedom is through the chimney (crematorium!). My job here is to introduce you to the new way of life: obedience, making of beds, marching, singing. (GA/mmm-archives)

Gutmann, as many former Dachau prisoners have confirmed, was in spite of all not a bad man, even though he sometimes howled, in fact, had to howl, with the pack. He often held philosophical discussions with Father Joseph Kentenich (the founder of the Schönstadt movement had to remain half a year, instead of the usual two weeks, in the infamous admissions barracks before he could move to the priests' barracks). Two times he even saved him from the invalid transport (from Dachau to Schloß Hartheim for gassing), which meant certain death.

Sometimes the old Dachau veterans gave the "newcomers" practical pointers, tips to survive. One hand rule was: "Never stand out! Never stand on the outer corners of a group! Disappear rather in the crowd! Never say that you are innocent, but rather willingly admit to something! Remember, the future belongs to the unnoticed!"

Sometimes prisoners fled to the toilets when an SS man approached. There they put their heads between their hands and stared at the floor. The SS men rarely entered the toilets. Thus many a prisoner was able to save himself from the harassment of the guards.

6

FIRST LETTERS FROM PRISON

The prisoners could write and receive only two letters a month from their relatives. That was one of the regulations "hammered into" the prisoners from the moment they entered the concentration camp. It was also sometimes printed on the letter paper which was sent to friends and relatives.

Every letter to relatives had to have the name, date of birth, and prison number of the writer. Furthermore, he always had to begin with the stereotyped statement: "I am doing well, I am healthy." Later on this was not taken so seriously.

The prisoners were strictly forbidden to report anything about camp life, even by allusion. In addition, they always had to send their letters to the *same* person, that is, either to their father, their mother, or one of their brothers or sisters. They could not change from one to the other.

Every letter went through the camp censor. If anything "suspicious" was found in it, the letter was immediately destroyed and the sender received the empty envelope back. If a prisoner received more mail than was allowed, the letters were sent back with the remark: "mail already received." It was likewise forbidden to quote Bible verses or refer to them. One prisoner, as a former inmate reports, was forbidden to write because he quoted a Bible verse. The prohibition lasted as long as he was in prison.

A further rule was that the letters had to be written on specially prepared concentration camp paper and had to be in German. "Letters were destroyed if written poorly or the contents were not clear enough. You could receive a penalty or lose your writing privileges for not writing a letter according to regulations" (J. Neuhäusler, *Wie war das im KZ Dachau?*).

Relatives could send a prisoner forty German marks a month, but no packages, because, as the official statement said, "the prisoners can buy everything in the camp." To this Sales Hess remarks: "This dirty lie stood printed on the camp stationery which went to our relatives for years, although there was almost nothing to buy in the canteen" (ibid.).

Whoever smuggled letters out of the camp was punished severely, even with death. In spite of this regulation, letters were smuggled out of prison from time to time. "With the passage of time, we also learned to write secret letters, and SS men were found who dropped the letters in the mail for us in Munich, although this was strictly forbidden" (Ernst Wilm).

Father Engelmar also succeeded in smuggling several letters out of the camp through an SS man (Franz Waldes) who was from Greifendorf. Hubert Unzeitig had attended grade school with him in Greifendorf. His sister Maria-Huberta passed these letters on to the Mariannhill Fathers in Riedegg, where they were then either destroyed or so carefully hidden that they could not be found again. It was too risky, in fact, mortally dangerous, to possess illegal letters from a concentration camp.

In these letters, as Father Otto Heberling (at that time local and provincial superior in Riedegg) remembers, Father Engelmar talked about life in the concentration camp, the daily roll calls, the long tiring periods of standing in wind and weather, the little food, the often unaccustomed work, the sicknesses, and the deaths. He mentioned the humiliating harassments, unsuccessful escape attempts, and subsequent severe punishments very cryptically and only by allusion.

"I Am Anxiously Awaiting News"

Almost all of the prisoners who wrote to their relatives used pseudonyms. Father Engelmar did the same. He called himself "Walter" in many letters, especially when he wanted to say something about himself without raising the suspicions of the censors.

From the first letters of Father Engelmar (June to December 1941), one can sense how much he was concerned about his relatives

and his former parish in Glöckelberg. A continual correspondence
with his sister Maria-Huberta was very important to him. She was,
you see, his only contact with the outside world through whom he
could have news about his family and his confreres.

The first letter which Father Engelmar wrote from Dachau carries
the date of June 15, 1941, which means it was written two weeks
after his admission. In the upper right hand corner is the prescribed
information about the prisoner: "Unzeitig Hubert, born on March
1, 1911, prisoner number 26 147, Barracks 26/2, Dachau K." There
follow date, greeting, and the first two sentences which we know
already: "I arrived here in Dachau on June 3. I am healthy." Then
he asks whether Maria has received his small suitcase with his
"things" from Linz, and then goes on: "What do you intend to
do in the future? Does Fr. Ansbert [his successor in the parish of
Glöckelberg—ed.] already have someone as housekeeper, and how
is he doing?" Finally he straightens out a few things about the Mass
intentions book (Mass intentions which were left over in Glöckelberg
when he was arrested) and then writes: "When you go home, tell
mother that I am still healthy and that I wanted to say good-bye in
Glöckelberg and that I was then quickly drafted. . . . Write me a
long letter soon about things at home, etc., and write also to Fr.
Otto [Heberling] that I can only write to one address. One of us
priests who has permission says a Mass for us every day; we also
have several breviaries here" (BAD 15.6.41).

The second letter is from June 29, 1941: "I have been waiting
anxiously for news from you. I wrote to you already from prison in
Linz on the back of the money-order form and now from the camp
(fourteen days ago), but have not received an answer. . . . Now, how
are all the dear relatives, especially mother? I am healthy and the
remaining eighty marks have been sent to me from the prison, so
that I can now buy myself something for my bread, writing materi-
als, etc. The money will be enough for me for several months, since
I get enough to eat here otherwise. Therefore, don't send me anything. Please write to me often and keep Fr. Otto informed about
me. . . . I am often with you in spirit, and especially in prayer I am
united with you. The thought strengthens all of us that not even a
hair falls from our head without the permission of God and that
everything works for the good of those who love God, or at least are
trying to love Him. Now, very sincere greetings to all dear relatives

and acquaintances, and do write often to your far distant brother Hubert" (BAD 29.6.41).

In his next letter, Father Engelmar asks again how Father Ansbert is doing, whether he has found a housekeeper, how it is going with the Mass intentions (he takes the matter scrupulously and wants to be of service to his successor in every way), and evidently he himself is still very attached to his former work. He ends the letter with the sentence: "Let us continue to pray and sacrifice for each other and for the salvation of mankind for Christ. Sincere thanks and greetings to all from Hubert" (BAD 13.7.41).

Two weeks later, Father Engelmar writes in another letter (in which he addresses the whole family): "I am happy that Maria answers my letters so punctually. She will have left, I presume, the somewhat inhospitable Glöckelberg with a feeling of relief. We certainly all want to pray and sacrifice for Fr. Ansbert that he will be able to persevere in this difficult place, if he intends to stay there. . . . Maria should send me as much news as she can about the relatives, the confreres in Riedegg and Würzburg, etc. . . . I presume the harvest will begin soon. Does the grain look good? We do not get out of the camp for work, so I do not know how it is here. We carry food in kettles from the kitchen to the others in the [thirty] individual barracks" (BAD 27.7.41).

With the last "smuggled in" sentence about carrying kettles, Father Engelmar alludes to something really bad, that is, the clergymen were sometimes condemned to perform this harassing work for all of the camp inhabitants. It was a murderous job, as we will learn later from eyewitnesses.

The letter written on August 10, 1941, begins with a little "peculiarity." On the letterhead with the address of the sender, after "Dachau, 3 K," there stand the words "concentration camp," written small but very clearly. The camp censor must have overlooked it. Father Engelmar asks his sister to be sure and always "write him back as soon as possible." Once again he asks information about various things: whether his clock (from the prison in Linz) has already arrived in Riedegg and whether everything has been regulated with the Mass intentions; whether Maria can send him five marks next time. He was very happy with the "comforting words from Sister Adelhilde" (his blood sister Regina who had been with the Mariannhill Missionary Sisters of the Precious Blood in Wernberg,

Carinthia, since 1937). "Mother will now have more peace because Maria is at home. She no longer has the worry about her child who lives far away. God directs everything with wonderful wisdom. We just don't always know immediately what everything is good for. I should like to thank Maria here for the loving care which she gave me in Glöckelberg and has given me since then. God will reward her and you, dear mother, for your love and care" (BAD 10.8.41).

"I Have Also Not Had a Cold So Far"

Repeatedly Father Engelmar asks about his other relatives, his confreres in Germany and Austria, and once in a while he puts in a few sentences about the camp or the conditions there, such as: "It often rains here. We have a library here, in addition, about two and a half hours of sleep twice a day, mornings and afternoons" (BAD 24.8.41).

Or he talks about the health of the relatives: "You are all healthy. So am I, thank God. Our daily order—up early and to bed early, change between carrying of food, Holy Mass, meals, sleep, afternoon prayer (since the beginning of September beautiful sunny weather for it again), Divine Office, etc. makes the time go by fast. Days and weeks just go by. One quarter of a year is already over. I try to use the time here as best I can for my spiritual, religious, and mental perfection. Prayer and reparation do not stand last on my program. I recommend you fervently to God every day at Holy Mass and pray for you on your feast days, etc." (BAD 7.9.41).

In the next letter, we read: "I have not yet seen any acquaintance from home, since we do not have any contact with the outside world. Only the guardian of the Franciscans from Moravian Trübau is in my barracks. He is from the Rhineland. Fr. Lenz is in m—." The sentence ends in the middle of a word. The camp censors cut the next two lines out. We do not know what Father Engelmar wrote. Probably it was an allusion to the sister of Father Johannes Maria Lenz, S.J., who had joined the Mariannhill Mission Sisters and thereby created an additional "bond" between the Mariannhillers and the Jesuits. (As is well known, Father Lenz survived the concentration camp in Dachau and later reported very extensively about

Father Engelmar. We will quote him frequently, especially in connection with the typhus barracks.)

In his letter from the beginning of October 1941, Father Engelmar speaks briefly about the weather. In September it was beautiful and sunny. "Now we should take the sweaters out from our things to use, and we will also soon receive socks for our wooden slippers, so I do not need anything else. (Nothing may be sent to us anyway.)" (BAD 5.10.41).

These short allusions speak volumes. The prisoners had nothing warm to wear, no socks and only wooden clogs, and it was not allowed to send them anything at all! In the same letter, we read: "I still feel healthy, thank God. I have not caught a cold so far either. The month of the rosary finds us gathered around the altar in the afternoon for a rosary in common to greet Mary, Help of Christians, Mediatrix of Graces, and to call on her motherly intercession. We also pray and sacrifice with St. Thérèse, Patroness of the Missions, for the spread of the great kingdom of souls of Christ the King, whom we want to honor at the end of the month of October."

In a letter written two weeks later, Father Engelmar takes up again the topic of his sweater and socks: "Once again we have cold, damp weather. But with the help of my sweater, which I have pulled out of my things, I can hold out. We will also soon receive socks, I think. The forty marks from you have arrived. I won't need any more until December. Please send me five stamps again next time. . . . What is the name of the man from Greifendorf who is here in the army? Circumstances permitting, he could come to visit me, since I cannot visit him. A certain assistant pastor Linhart from Landskron is also here" (BAD 19.10.41). So for the first time, we hear a hidden allusion to the SS man from Greifendorf (Franz Waldes), who, as we mentioned above, smuggled several letters out of Dachau.

As can be seen, small, important pieces of information, skillfully hidden, are scattered among other unimportant matters. Between information about the weather, a remark is made about clothing. Among comments about books and health, something is "strewn in" about prayer life in the camp. This was the only way possible to get letters through the censors. Prisoners and SS men in charge of the censorship had to be outwitted as inconspicuously as possible!

A former priest inmate of a concentration camp, to quote one last example, had a very special method to get information out of the camp: "I had developed another secret formula with a companion who came from my home town and whose mother lived close to us. I wrote only half sentences. My companion wrote the other half. When the two mothers, who had quickly caught on, put the two letters together, they got the full news."

7

PRIESTS' BARRACKS NO. 26

Dachau was the "biggest monastery in the world" (J. Lenz, *Christus in Dachau*). Nearly 3,000 clergymen lived there in the closest proximity. There had never been such a large collection of—predominantly Catholic—clergy which lived, worked, and prayed together so closely and for so long.

The *Dachau Documentation* published by the International Committee of Dachau (Brussels) shows that, of the total 2,720 clergy in the Dachau concentration camp, 2,579 were Catholics and 109 Protestant. The rest were Orthodox, Muslims, Old Catholics, and Mariavites (a national church sect in Poland). Of these 2,720 clergymen, 447 were Germans.

Eugene Weiler's (GID) figures are a little different. He gives proof of 228 German diocesan clergy, 70 German religious priests, and 35 non-Catholic clergy. He thereby arrives at a combined number of 333 German clergy. Probably the Germans from the rest of the Reich (Austrians, Germans from Czechoslovakia, etc.) must be added to that number to reach the number of the *Dachau Documentation*. According to Weiler, sixty-five Catholics and eight Protestants of the German clergy died in the concentration camp. Weiler says that the total number of clergy imprisoned in Dachau was 2,794.

On December 8, 1940, the clergy of all faiths was drawn together in Barracks Nos. 26, 28, and 30. These three barracks—they were particularly dangerous in the eyes of the SS—were also nicknamed for short "priests' barracks." They were surrounded by a special barbed wire fence and could be entered only by the clergy, not by other prisoners. "One of our own had to stand guard at the barracks gate during the day and could only let in 'clergymen'" (letter from

Father Richard Schneider to Father Bernstein regarding F. Averesch, *Redemptoristen Gedenkblätter* 1981).

From January 21, 1941, on, there was a chapel in Barracks 26 where a Mass could be celebrated daily. The chapel was a picture of poverty: the altar was of crate slats, the chalice was a metal bowl, and the tabernacle was made of tin cans. But it was enough to celebrate Mass.

Lay persons—and from September 19, 1941, on, the Polish clergy in Barracks 28 too—could not take part in the eucharistic celebration in the prison chapel. Nevertheless, individuals sneaked in from time to time. Mass was also often disturbed by ruthless SS men. The Polish priests also had to turn in their rosaries and Breviaries. The commander forbade them, under threat of the severest penalties, every religious practice, even within their own barracks. In spite of this, there was an active religious life in Barracks 28.

Mass was celebrated often at various places on the camp grounds, always, of course, without Mass vestments and candles and with a tin can or a water glass as chalice. The prisoners stood around a flower bed, or they squatted in the corner of a greenhouse, all the while watching out for the SS who could catch them.

Time and again, German priests succeeded in bringing hosts or particles of hosts to their Polish confreres or other prisoners, naturally always under great danger. Father Albert Riesterer of the Archdiocese of Freiburg writes: "Often I took a second host in my hand, carried it with me in a clean piece of paper to the plantation in order to be able to bring Communion to the poor Polish priests who had to do without this comfort. I had my tabernacle in a small fir tree" (FDA).

Dachau—a School of Prayer

Much praying was done in the priests' barracks. The clergymen said night prayer together every evening in the dormitory. They prayed for their parish communities and for their persecutors. And at the end of their prayer in common, they gave a common blessing to all their friends and enemies from their beds. Ernst Wilm, a Protestant pastor, adds the following comments about the prayer life in the Dachau priests' barracks: "In the evening, we all, Catholics and Protestants, prayed together in the dormitory. In the morning, after the Communist barracks elder had shouted, 'Everyone up!' one of the priests shouted, 'Praised be Jesus Christ!' And we answered in unison, 'Forever. Amen.' Then began the feverish and torturous day, but we were strengthened by the word of God and our prayer; that was our 'heaven' in Dachau!" (*So sind wir nun Botschafter*).

In an earlier work about Dachau, which we have quoted already, Wilm reports: "When I could not bear it any longer to be gathered with 180 to 200 other persons together in one room, I often went into the chapel to pray. . . . For when you are totally poor and helpless and can find no help from others, when you then learn to pour out your heart before God and ask him for everything, even little things, like a little warm sunshine for your freezing damp body, a piece of dry bread for your gnawing hunger, a pair of shoes that don't hurt your sore feet so much, a work which won't kill you . . . , yes, then you appreciate the gift of being able to pray."

The priests addressed many prayers to the Blessed Mother, for one day a statue of Mary turned up in the prison chapel. (It stands today in the chapel of the Carmelite monastery just behind the old barbed wire fence and watchtower.) Father Dominikus Hoffmeister, provincial of the Salvatorians, tells how it came to Dachau:

"During the war years, I was superior of our seminary in Jägerndorf (Czechoslovakia). A long-time wish was fulfilled one day when I was able to obtain a wooden statue of Our Lady in Breslau in order to give it a place of honor in our house chapel. Then the parish secretary told me that Bishop Nathan had the opportunity to get an image of Our Lady to the priests in Dachau. I frankly admit that it was not easy for me to part with the statue. We wrapped it in a blanket and pushed it on a sled—there was deep snow—to the rectory in Jägerndorf. Bishop Nathan saw to the transport of the precious statue to Dachau" (SvD 1/55).

Monsignor Georg Schelling tells how the statue got to the camp, was unpacked there and put up: "The package was brought to the priests' barracks like all other packages, and was checked there by the barracks leader. The same SS man on duty did not always come for this. When the barracks leader who had to check the packages on that day saw the package, his eyes grew large and he made a remark that it was hardly likely that it was a 'food package.' The package was opened and he saw the contents. He was not cross, but he remarked that he could not let the package in because it did not contain food, clothing, etc. I made the suggestion that the package should be put aside until the matter could be regulated. Later I brought it into the chapel 'because of lack of space in the living area.' The barracks leader who came the next day evidently did not know anything about it and did not ask about it. So the Blessed Mother was unpacked and put up. Afterwards not one person asked where the statue had come from" (SvD 10/68).

Around this time, the prayer of the Dachau priests to the Mother of God was composed. Its author was Father Johann Schulz, who died in August 1941. We reprint it here slightly abbreviated:

Our dear Lady of Dachau!

Although we ourselves are in need of comfort, we beg you: Go on holy pilgrimage and comfort all who need your help. It is war time, and millions suffer day and night from dangers to body and soul. Show that you are a mother and strengthen them. Millions have lost house and home and wander around without shelter among strangers. In that suffering which you yourself bore in your exile to Egypt, be for them refuge and strength. And in that great pain which you suffered under the cross, comfort the sick and wounded, give strength to prisoners, and in the hour of death stand by those who must sacrifice their blood and their life. . . . Bless and protect the bishops in their difficult office. Protect and support especially our Holy Father, the Pope, whose heart must be very heavy because he is powerless to remove the distress, lessen the suffering, and bring about peace. And when you, dear Lady of Dachau, come to those places where our parents and relatives, our parishioners and pastoral workers have been praying so long for our return, then tell them that you are watching over us in life and in death. Our dear Lady of Dachau, show that you are a mother where the need is greatest. Amen. (see M. Münch, *Unter 2579 Priestern in Dachau*)

Father Engelmar, who was a great devotee of Mary, said this prayer innumerable times and thought of his mother, his four sisters, his relatives, and his confreres while doing so. For him, Dachau was not only a path of suffering but also a school of prayer. He could relate to the words of Curt Goetz, who once said: "Love your destiny. It is God's walk with your soul."

As Maurus Münch has rightly said, to have been in Dachau does not mean much, but to have sought the way to God more intensively in Dachau, that was the real grace of those years. Therein lies redemption and a mission, he believes, "until the end of our life which has been given to us anew" (ibid.).

Special kinds of Torture

In itself, the daily order in the Dachau priests' barracks seemed rather humane. After rising (at 5:00 AM), there was washing, making of beds, breakfast, and roll call. Prime and Mass followed at 7:15. The prisoners were dispensed from the rules of eucharistic fast which still existed at that time. From 9:00 to 11:00 was study time in silence, followed by free time. Dinner was at 11:30. At 12:30 was midday rest, then Vespers and free time. The evening meal was at 17:00, roll call at 18:00, and finally bed time at 21:00.

That doesn't read like a concentration camp schedule. Unlike other prisoners, the clergy had it relatively "good." They could celebrate Mass and pray the Divine Office. There was even a "library" with a few books. What more could they want?

But the whole thing lasted only a year. Then the clergymen were assigned again to the work groups, especially to the "plantation." With that, the midday rest period was dropped and Mass had to be celebrated before the morning roll call. In addition, the clergymen were immediately exposed to special tortures.

There was, for example, the "wine torture." The clergymen had to drink a quarter liter of wine from an aluminum mug at the order of an SS man. Whoever choked on it, drank too slow, or could not finish it was beaten on the head and in the face. That was a terrible punishment!

An eyewitness account: "A special affair was made of the quarter liter of wine which every clergyman in Barracks 26 was entitled to from a bequest of the Holy Father. There were not to be any joys in this world without God, so the pleasure of a glass of wine also had to be made bitter. These wine bottles were counted exactly and delivered to the barracks in crates in the morning. When the barracks leader, an SS man, came, it was 'wine order' time. The bottles had to be opened before his eyes. The confreres sat down in prearranged groups of three. Each group received one bottle. The barracks leader ordered: 'Pour!' Everyone received a quarter liter in his aluminum mug. Then followed the order: 'Drain mugs!' The quarter liter had to be drunk in one draft, while sometimes the SS man drove the prisoners on to drink faster. Thereupon came the order: 'Show mugs!' Everyone had to turn his mug upside down and hold it up, so that not a drop would remain for reasonable drinking. Finally came the command: 'Mugs down!' With that the 'wine order' was over. The SS man picked the time for this order at his pleasure: it could be in the morning, before or after the meal" (S. Hess, ibid.).

Father Franz Goldschmitt describes the "wine order" even more drastically: "Everything was done amid much shouting. First the SS man shouted: 'Wine carriers forward!' Meanwhile the other clergymen each received a mug in their hands according to instructions. Absolute silence. Then again came the voice of the SS man: 'Are the clergymen ready to drink?' The unit elder shouted back: 'Yes, sir, Mister Barracks Leader!' Then the SS man shouted: 'Open the bottles!' Twenty bottles had to be opened at breakneck speed with two corkscrews. If it didn't go fast enough, the SS man gave out blows. Now the barracks leader climbed up on a stool. Every clergyman held his mug in his hand and looked up at the SS man. He then shouted: 'Drain it!' and paid close attention that everyone drained his mug completely and that all did it at the same time. Whoever choked on the wine, drank too slowly, or even could not finish it was beaten on the head and in the face. Sometimes the wine drinking was deliberately postponed. Then the next time every clergyman had to drink a double portion, i.e., a half liter in one draft, and that not rarely early in the morning on an empty stomach" (ibid.).

On February 11, 1942, the wine distribution with its commands was stopped. Another terrible torture was the carrying of the food kettles for all of the prisoners. That was a worse harassment than any slave labor. Two weakened and freezing priests, driven on by the shouts and blows of the SS, had to carry one cooking kettle between them.

Albert Riesterer describes it: "Some got a hernia from the work. The kettles were of iron with an iron lining, heavy already by themselves; to this was added the contents, about fifty liters of tea, coffee, or soup. All in all, seventy-five kilograms. Each kettle was carried by two men, but what kind of men! Weakened by hunger, frozen from long waiting, excited by blows received in the kitchen, wearing slippery wooden clogs, they had to run down five icy steps, through the snow and over ice-covered paths" (FDA).

Three times a day the kettles had to be carried, and that by men who often only weighed fifty kilograms! "Carrying these kettles was an accomplishment for strong, healthy men. It was a torture for skinny, starved ones. The kettles were shifted much from side to side; your hands, arms, back, and your feet in their wooden clogs all hurt" (Eugen Weiler/GID).

"Once," writes Father Hermann Dümig, "I forgot to take off my cap in the SS kitchen as I ran to the food kettles. Pow! I received a blow on the head which made me lose my hearing and sight. I could just barely hold on to the kettle to keep it from spilling. You were under continual tension. . . . If the contents of a kettle were spilled, the priests' barracks had to sacrifice one of its kettles—and had to go without. There were no substitutes" (GA/mmm-archives).

An equally hard torture was snow shoveling in winter. Dachau, which lies at 700 meters on the edge of the Alps, often had long and snowy winters. Every time snow fell, "snow orders" were given and the clergymen had to go to work.

One former prisoner remembered it: "One night before Epiphany, an enormous amount of damp snow fell. Early in the morning about 3:30, the inhabitants of the priests' barracks were awakened by the command: 'Everyone out! Shovel snow!' The work went on for many days. It was a hard and awful work. There were not enough shovels and wheelbarrows, so the snow had to be carried away on tabletops and even in pieces of clothing" (Zeuch/SvD 4/57).

Jean Bernard describes the scene even more extensively: "The first days of January 1942 brought gigantic amounts of snow. The thermometer went down to 20–30 degrees below zero. From morning until evening, snow was collected, shoveled, and brought to the creek in wheelbarrows. More than 1,000 clergymen were put to work, while the SS and the leaders kept us running with blows and kicks. . . . Everything had to be done on the run. I fell over my wheelbarrow through exhaustion and needed time to straighten up. An SS man jumped up and ordered me to run with the load. He then ran next to me and kept hitting me with a thong.

"When I got to the creek, I was not allowed to stop, but had to take the load around a second time. When he left me and I set the wheelbarrow down, my hand was frozen to it and I had to free it with the help of my warm breath. . . . Because there were not enough wheelbarrows, some of us were ordered to bring the table-tops from our barracks. These were piled with snow and then carried away by four men on their shoulders" (ibid.).

That was forced labor of the worst kind! What luck—in as far as you can even speak of luck in this context—that the "snow brigade" only lasted for a couple of months in the year!

8

FORCED LABOR
ON THE PLANTATION

From April 1942 on, the clergy did extremely hard work on the so-called plantation ("Dachau swamp"), a piece of land which comprised several hundred acres. On the plantation, pepper, paprika, bean tressel, basil, and thyme were grown. In addition, various drugs were produced and vitamins were extracted from gladioli leaves. Large experimental fields were connected to the plantation.

On these spice and medicinal herb fields of the SS, the prisoners had to do very hard work. By the hundreds they pushed along on their knees, pulled weeds, and crawled through water channels which smelled like the plague, with no protection from wind and rain, nor from the *kapos* who often treated them like animals. And all this was done under continual pressure, without a pause, often at a running pace, and always under threat of blows.

In addition, there was the terrible hunger! In contrast to the other prisoners (including foreigners and Russians), the clergymen did not have a "snack" on the plantation. Work outdoors was not ranked as hard work by the SS. For that reason, there was no bread for the clergy, but only work.

Jean Bernard describes how hungry the prisoners were and how hard they tried, for example, to get their hands on something "green" under great risk: "For days on the way home, I had watched a juicy dandelion on the side of the road. Many others stared at it, too, wondering how they could get it. I had made up my mind that the dandelion would be mine! One day when the *kapo* was on the other side of the column and I was marching on the outer edge, I suddenly threw my cap over the yellow flower as I went by, jumped from my place, tore the plant out together with my cap, and pushed the whole lot down on my head" (ibid.).

Once—in the fall of 1942—an extra portion of bread was given out. The prisoners were overjoyed. "Some ate it immediately, others saved it, holding it respectfully in their hands like a gift from heaven" (Franz Weinmann). Food was Question No. 1 in the concentration camp. People who have never hungered cannot even imagine what this means.

Almost daily, prisoners collapsed from carrying loads that were too heavy or from pushing wheelbarrows on the run. "If someone took a breathing spell, he was either knocked down on the spot for laziness or even 'refusal to work,' or he was punished back at the barracks in the usual way" (W. Adam, *Nacht über Deutschland*).

Probably most of the clergymen who died in the Dachau concentration camp owe their early death to the terrible treatment on the plantation. The exhausted and completely starved men were treated like slaves, and sometimes worse than animals. They were harnessed like oxen or horses to plows and harrows, six men numbly pulled the heavy loads. Others had to carry water, collect tea or dry herbs— at 120 degrees or more. Still others had to grind the herbs and got sore eyes or filled their lungs with dust while doing so.

The clergymen did not wear any kind of protective clothing in this work on the concentration camp fields, not even in the worst weather. "Even putting down a piece of cardboard on the soaked ground to kneel on was severely punished" (S. Hess).

In such an environment, it was hard to keep one's trust in the goodness and love of God. That the clergymen did so, in spite of everything, was due not only to their vocation and their training, it was also due to a certain amount of personal experience of God in Dachau, which time and again gave them wings and kept them from despairing.

Hans Brantzen from the Diocese of Mainz speaks very movingly of Father Engelmar in this regard. They got to know one another in the priests' barracks in November 1941. From April 1942 on, they worked together on the plantation. In a letter to the Mariannhill Missionaries in Würzburg, Brantzen writes:

"I got acquainted with Unzeitig as a co-worker in Greenhouse 6 of the infamous plantation. They were terrible months—in heat, rain, and snow. We had to push wheelbarrows and dig up beds. We sat on the transplant beds in rain and storm, Unzeitig and I often together. Without having to eulogize, I can safely say: he was always the same. When others complained and thought of the good old days, when it became too much for them and they could not go on, he looked up to his Father. And it helped. The main qualities of his fine personality were modesty, quietness, and a peaceable disposition in the closeness of the barracks. All that, however, did not make him stand out. What did stand out was his charity when he begged for the other poor prisoners from his confreres. . . . How often after the frugal evening meal, he sat before his book *Workday Holiness* and copied out excerpts, which I often discussed with him. Both of us belonged to a small circle which discussed liturgical, homiletic, and pastoral problems. He never missed a chance for adoration of the Blessed Sacrament in his free time. When we came back to our barracks, tired from the hard work, to eat our portion of turnips or something else, he would go into the chapel before entering the living area. In the evening, Unzeitig could always be seen in the chapel for a few minutes. The same was true before every activity. With the greatest heroism, he kept going through the death summer and hunger months of 1942, although he was often so tired and weak that he could have fallen over, as we all were. Through it all, he remained the same helpful and quiet man he always was" (FN 1/1950).

9

LETTERS FROM 1941–1942

If we study the letters written by Father Engelmar in the concentration camp, we notice how again and again he looks for comfort and refuge in faith. Dachau was for him, as for the other clergymen imprisoned there, a school of life and a school of prayer. His letters from 1941 and 1942, which he mostly wrote to his sister Maria-Huberta every fourteen days, show this in a special way.

In one letter, written in the middle of December 1941, he writes: "What sometimes appears as misfortune is often the greatest fortune. How much a person learns only through experience in the school of life. We should feel and experience for others, I think, the lack of peace in the world and help them to true peace. Then we are not surprised if God takes from us some things which are dear and precious to us" (BAD 15.12.41).

At the beginning of the same letter, Father Engelmar wishes his loved ones the peace of the coming feast of Christmas: "Christ, too, knocks on the doors of the world and wants to give it peace. But it seems that today the waves of division are washing too high for a general peace to be possible. All the guilt and injustice which human evil and limitation have heaped up is also not yet atoned for. If it already seems that God's hand is laid upon us, then let us believe that we are contributing to the atonement for guilt and fault."

These lines reveal the religious moorings of the Mariannhill priest. Father Engelmar, in the totally desperate desolation of the Dachau concentration camp, felt like Fyodor Dostoyevsky. The Russian poet, who knew the penal camps of the czars from personal experience, writes in his memoirs: "In the desolation of forced labor, one thirsts for faith as dry grass thirsts for rain—and finally one finds it because it stands out much clearer in misfortune. . . . Perhaps the Almighty sent me here so that I could learn the essence of all things and teach it to others. Those who are prisoners of guilt and misfortune need love more than the innocent and happy."

In two other letters, the missionary zeal of Father Engelmar comes out especially. He always, even in the concentration camp, felt himself to be a missionary. If he could not teach souls, then he wanted, according to a saying of Saint Thérèse of Lisieux, at least to suffer and do penance for them.

On January 11, 1942, he wrote: "A saying of Saint Thérèse gives me great comfort: 'With words, it is true, souls can be instructed, but they can only be saved by suffering!' I wish very much in this way to be able to come somewhat to the assistance of Fr. Ansb. [Father Ansbert in Glöckelberg—ed.]."

At the end of 1942, he writes: "We daily notice here on ourselves that many prayers are being offered for us and that God directs everything wonderfully. However, I hope, as I already said, that I will also be able to work here for eternity. . . . Only when one stands all by himself does he see how far he has come in spiritual improvement. There are opportunities everywhere for experience and stimulation" (BAD 25.1.42).

Repeatedly Father Engelmar alludes to the harassments which he and his confreres in the concentration camp had to put up with: "Walter [his alias—ed.] could tell you something about how the devil stirs up storm and disturbance over and over when many souls are again snatched from his power in the time before Easter, and how this battle and fury increases in the time when Christ's way of suffering reached its zenith" (BAD 5.4.42).

In another letter, we read: "I am convinced that God will preserve Walter even without the help of his relatives, if He has work for him in the future. If not, the saying holds: What God does is done well. Some of his companions have probably passed over into eternity already. God has accepted the sacrifice of their lives" (BAD 28.6.42).

Those are very clear indications of the inhuman hardships on the plantation, which he was forbidden to write about. The words of his next letter are even clearer and more emphatic: "Certainly God has also heard your prayers for Walter, who has also had to go through hard times. Recently he thought that, if Maria were still with him, she would not have half the work, not so much to prepare, to clean, etc., since he is now already satisfied with half as much. That's how unassuming he has become. I hope his health holds up" (BAD 12.7.42).

In several letters, there is a light undertone of hope that perhaps, in spite of all, he would be released at the end of the time of suffering, if God so willed: "God is really good and does not desert anyone who trusts in Him, even if He lets bitterly hard times come upon some persons. It is, I think, a time of exertion of all energies in the world. Let us hope for the establishment of a prompt and lasting peace, a peace of love and understanding for the purification and improvement of hearts and souls. Yes, as Walter recently thought, if this hope did not exist, one would have to go crazy in all the distress of body and soul, but God's ruling of the world is not senseless and heartless, as some people are. But Walter in the Far North should only take courage, what he certainly is trying to do over and over again in spite of all discouragement. . . . Let us hope that grain and fruit will result from a somewhat good harvest, so that the specter of hunger will be abolished and God will also again have mercy on those who are dependent on the will of others for every bit of bread" (BAD 25.7.42).

These lines are from the time of terrible hunger in the camp, which will be described in the next chapter. The camouflaged news about his own hunger and discouragement cannot be overheard. The following letter from August 9, 1942, Father Engelmar ended with the words: "Let us pray together for Walter that God have mercy on him and change his lot!"

Again and again, Father Engelmar asks about the health of his mother and the welfare of his relatives, friends, and confreres. He shows his gratitude for the letters received and for the monthly gifts of forty marks. Most of the time, his religious words of encouragement go to his loved ones at home. They reveal him again and again as a pious and holy priest: "If only people would find the way back to God through this shocking sermon and would not seek their salvation any more in earthly means of power! It hurts one to see a whole people heading for the abyss" (BAD, without date).

In summary, it may be said that almost all the letter excerpts clearly show how much not only Father Engelmar but all the prisoners had to suffer under the forced labor in the concentration camp. At that time, between 12,000 and 15,000 men stood in the service of the SS in Dachau.

Family photo from the year 1927. Hubert was 16. *Left to right:* Hubert's sisters Else and Emilie, Hubert, his mother, his maternal grandfather, and his sisters Maria (Sr. Huberta) and Regina (Sr. Adelhilde).

Father Engelmar's First Mass in Greifendorf. With Father Engelmar are his mother and three of his sisters.

The street in front of Barracks 26.

Mass in the chapel of Barracks 26.

The concentration camp at Dachau today.
The stone block marks the location of Barracks 26, one of the
so-called priests' barracks.

Memorial in Dachau: "To Honor the Dead. To Warn the Living."

10

SUMMER OF HUNGER 1942

In the summer of 1942, a genuine famine broke out in the Dachau concentration camp, and also among the clergy of Barracks No. 26. For the hard work which had to be done on the plantation from morning until night, the food was simply too little. Black coffee (imitation), water soup (with cabbage leaves, turnips, or stinging nettle), a couple of potatoes, once in a while a small piece of margarine or a small slice of sausage were not enough. This led increasingly to weakness and exhaustion.

In addition, the prisoners did not have sufficient clothing and had to remain outside in the cold and the heat, in all kinds of bad weather. Hermann Dümig writes: "From the end of April until the end of August 1942, our activity was almost exclusively pulling weeds on our knees mornings and afternoons in all kinds of weather without tools, so that our fingernails, which had already grown thinner because of the lack of food, did not need to be manicured anymore. . . . Our clothing had to dry on our backs, since we did not have a second set to change into" (GA/mmm archives, Cologne).

Father Otto Pies reports about the famine of 1942: "More than all the others, the many hundreds of priests in the concentration camp had to suffer terribly because they were employed in hard work without receiving the additional food which the other prisoners were given for their work time. The water soup and the small piece of bread, with five or six potatoes, did not suffice to maintain strength. Every day one or two priests collapsed from weakness and died two days later" (*Helfende Hände*).

Pastor Richard Schneider adds: "Because of the poor, insufficient diet, the prisoners tried to get their hands on anything edible: grass,

leaves, leeks, parsley—anything which could be found on the plantation. This diet only increased the number of persons sick from starvation and contributed substantially to the great number of deaths
among the clergy. The high number of priests' deaths began with
the Polish clergy in June 1942 and the German clergy in July 1942"
(FDA 90/1970).

Diarrhea and edema caused by starvation continued to grow in
the camp. According to Father Johannes Maria Lenz, there was
hardly a Dachau prisoner in 1942 who, because of hunger, had not
had ordinary diarrhea or dysentery. The first signs were usually
chills and gas. The only remedy would have been—to eat absolutely
nothing! But who still had the will power to do that? Starvation
reaped its harvest with time. More and more prisoners got seriously
sick. First the feet and legs swelled. (Some propped up their legs,
but often that did not help anymore either.) Then the arms, hands,
and head also swelled and people had a constant diarrhea, a kind of
"hunger and typhus diarrhea."

Among the deaths that summer was also that of the diocesan
priest Father Georg Häfner (pastor in Oberschwarzach) of the Diocese of Würzburg. Sales Hess writes about him: "He came to the
camp several months after me. His crime was that he had announced
from the pulpit that someone on his deathbed had brought his ir-
regular marriage in order. . . . The Nazis held this announcement
against him and reported him as a disturber of the peace, and had
him sent to Dachau. . . . The specter of starvation took hold of him
in August 1942. His feet, hands, and head showed the usual swell-
ing. When I saw him for the last time, his eyes were already all
swollen up. Shortly before his death, he got a phlegmon, one of
those pussy inflammations of the connective tissue, which for a time
had gone around like a plague in Dachau, but by that time had
almost disappeared. A few days later, the announcement of his death
arrived" (ibid.).

Starvation brought numerous prisoners to a miserable death.
"Fifty-five out of two hundred and fifty-five confreres died that year.
The percentage among the Polish priests and the religious was substantially higher—all together about 800 victims in 1942!" (Hermann Dümig)

The months of starvation were a terrible and desolate time for
the prisoners. During this time, everything, but everything, turned

around the topic of eating. Other topics (politics, culture, religion) became secondary and unimportant. Everyone had only one problem: How can I get something to eat? What is lying around that could be eaten: roots, herbs, grasses, dandelions, lamb's lettuce, rhubarb, sorrel, and so on?

As much as twenty marks were given for one single piece of bread. But even at that, bread was a scarce commodity. In the fight over the small amount of food, it came repeatedly to terrible and macabre scenes among the prisoners. Lew Kopelew is right when he writes: "Hunger is worse than death."

Food Packages from Home

In the fall of 1942, there came the long-awaited permission allowing the prisoners to have food packages shipped from home. This was a blessing that can hardly be described. For otherwise, thousands of additional prisoners would have died from the consequences of starvation.

It is not completely clear what caused the SS finally to grant this mitigation. Certainly it was not humane, but rather "war-related," motives which had led to such a decision. The prisoners were needed for the war industry—as work slaves. Starving prisoners could not be good workers.

Whatever the motives were, a big campaign of sending packages to Dachau began. "At times, over one hundred packages a day came to the living quarters," writes Father Sales Hess. Many people's lives were saved by this help.

Since the Polish and other prisoners from the East only received a few packages, the German and Austrian clergymen helped out. They distri buted much food to other barracks. Now even those who had prejudices against the priests gradually lost their deep seated animosities.

The sick in the "medical center" (hospital barracks in the concentration camp) likewise received much food from Barracks No. 26. "A real charity service was organized. In every living area, cartons stood up front near the window where we could put cakes, apples, and other things desired by the sick. Every day, the orderlies carried big, heavy packages to the hospital" (S. Hess, ibid.).

Hans Karl adds: "Everyone of us had several poor compatriots from his hometown whom he wanted to help. Often one or another could be seen leaving the barracks with small packages in order to distribute his gifts. Morning, noon, and night, many beggars stood at the gates of Barracks No. 26. They were hungry and asked for a piece of bread. They were given much. . . . It was unknown to the camp public how much (good) was secretly done. Some went by the principle to help only their countrymen; the attitude of most, however, was to help only the needy. The Dutch took care of their poor Dutch compatriots; the Czechs and especially the Polish, the compatriots of their nation. In 1943, when the misery grew especially among the TB patients, we decided to give up our whole bread ration every Thursday and give it to the sick. In addition, each unit collected food every day and turned it over to the hospital. Each one also often gave a sum from his canteen account for a common purchase for other barracks in which companions lived who didn't receive packages. We bought and gave away whole barrels of (red) beets" (ibid.).

The clergymen helped many prisoners in the concentration camp with their generosity. Their reputation grew even among the Communists of the camp. Theodor Brasse states, regarding occasional accusations that the clergymen had lacked the necessary helpfulness and solidarity: "The fact is, that through the charitable activity of the clergymen, the nutrition and health level in the camp was raised and the number of deaths for a time was reduced to a normal amount" (quoted by Eugen Weiler, GID).

Because a part of the food which came into the camp by package needed to be prepared, a "cooking corner" was set up in Barracks No. 26. "Most of the preparation was done by clergymen who, because of age or physical handicap, were no longer assigned to work. The joke about the 'cooking church' now went about the barracks. Many lay people who entered the barracks on Sundays [in the last years of the war this was more possible than in the first years, although it was still not allowed—ed.] were thus able to enjoy coffee and tea with something to eat. It must be admitted that there were a few who could not part with anything they had, that human, all too human, things also occurred among the clergy. But isn't heroism also a grace?" (Theodor Brasse)

Not Forgotten in Exile

Father Engelmar reacted joyfully to the first package, which reached him in October-November 1942. Since the letters of this period are undated, the exact date can no longer be established. Among other things, he writes: "I see that we are not forgotten here in exile."

Father Engelmar accepted thankfully every package which he subsequently received from his mother and sister, but also from the Mariannhill Fathers in Reimlingen. Now packages could also be received from other persons, although the prisoners themselves could still write to only one address.

From a thank-you letter of January 1943, we see that Father Engelmar considered it a duty of love to share his packages with other concentration camp prisoners: "It depends on us to do everything for the glory of God, and to make others happy. Then we have the greatest profit and life becomes more bearable. In this sense, I also consider the use of the charitable gifts which dear people send to us in our seclusion, because not everyone is so lucky as to receive something" (BAD).

In another letter, Father Engelmar worries that his loved ones at home could do too much good and take treats out of their own mouths: "It is really touching that you want to, and do, send me so much; I would like to ask you, however, to let up, because I do not want to live a nice life at your expense. The times are too serious for that, and mother's sick nerves need good nourishment. My health is very good, thank God. Will try to hold out bravely and continue to do only God's will and to offer up all praying and penance for a blessed apostolate of my confreres" (BAD 24.1.43).

When Father Engelmar received by telegram the news of the unexpected death of his mother, he wrote to his sister on March 21, 1943: "Although I was not able to see mother anymore in this life [Father Engelmar had seen her for the last time when he returned to Würzburg at the beginning of September 1939 after his First Mass!—ed.], it is nevertheless a great consolation to me that you, dear sister, remained faithful to your heroic decision and nursed mother so well until she died. Write to me, please, more about her sudden death. God will richly reward your loyal love and, now that you are alone,

He will not desert you and will give you the right decision for the future" (BAD).

For his deceased mother, Father Engelmar was able to say a Requiem Mass in Dachau. It was the first Mass since his imprisonment which he could celebrate himself, one of the few Masses which he said in his four years of concentration camp.

The letters which Father Engelmar wrote from Dachau after that dealt with various topics. Among other things, we hear about the final profession of his sister Regina (Sr. Adelhilde) on May 31, 1943, in Wernberg, the remembrance of Father Engelmar's First Mass on August 15, and the bombing of Munich during the night of October 3, 1943, when an incendiary bomb fell on the concentration camp and ignited the roof of the administration building, destroying the so-called "personal effects storage room" (with the personal possessions of the prisoners).

Again and again, Father Engelmar begs his beloved ones not to make too many sacrifices for his sake: "Whatever you do, don't rob yourself too much of necessities! I would not really like it if you lack anything at all" (BAD 3.10.43). Now he often signs his letters with "Hubert far away." The long years of separation from home are an additional sacrifice for him.

From Hans Brantzen, we know that from about the middle of 1943 Father Engelmar was no longer working on the plantation but in the pay station of the combat SS outside of the concentration camp. Among other things, Brantzen writes about the relationship of Father Engelmar to his superiors:

"By means of his reserved, irreproachable conduct, he won such an influence over his SS leader, a veteran lieutenant platoon leader, that the lieutenant often held more serious conversations with him. Yes, Unzeitig could even write this SS man personal letters and work on him in other ways. It was a very peculiar relationship, almost a mystery, how Fr. Engelmar's deeply spiritual, priestly conduct influenced this person, who up until then had been far from the Church. It will probably always remain a secret what the two finally talked about and how deeply Fr. Unzeitig influenced the future of this man" (FN 1/1950).

In a letter of October 17, 1943, Father Engelmar mentioned his work in the SS pay station for the first time: "As I have found out, Walter is still working in the government office. So he can manage.

He would rather, of course, help you or use his physical and mental energies somewhere else, but he tries to make a virtue out of necessity and use everything for the purposes of his supreme Lord. . . . I thank God for every day which He gives me in order to show him in some way love and gratitude for His countless benefits. One notices more and more each day that all His arrangements and guidance is pure love. And daily I beg Him: Father, have mercy on your children. Bring to an end the gruesome murder and grant us Your peace, the peace which only You can give" (BAD).

11

HARASSMENT
ON HARASSMENT

By means of the food packages, Father Engelmar, his clerical confreres, and the other concentration camp prisoners in Dachau had more and better food to eat again, but the harassments of the SS continued. And these harassments were terrible, inhuman, as the following examples show.

For a long time, Father Otto Pies writes in his book *Stephanus heute*, all clergymen, after they were admitted to the camp, were immediately brought to the penalty barracks where they were strictly isolated, put to very hard work, and harassed even to the point of being threatened with death. That changed only when the war broke out.

Camp Commander Hoffmann occasionally greeted the newcomers in the Dachau Jourhaus with the words: "Even if the war should be lost, we still have enough time to drive you all into the electrical barbed wire!" (quoted by Brantzen, GID).

Beside the various disciplinary works (in the "penal company"), the following punishments were most feared: hanging on the tree, twenty-five double lashes, which sometimes were given outside in front of all the prisoners, and the standing cell. The last (according to Hans Carls, fifty by fifty-four centimeters and 2.10 meters high) was a torture of a special kind. The prisoner had to stay in it for two weeks, on bread and water. Sadistic guards, by means of needle points, kept the tortured prisoner from sitting.

Johann Neuhäusler describes the twenty-five double lashes on the rack prescribed in Dachau: "It pleased the guards when the prisoner

screamed, wept, howled, or fainted from pain. . . . Shortly before
the penalty, the prisoner was told that he must conscientiously count
the lashes. If, because of the pain, he forgot to count, the SS men
explained, they would not know how many lashes he had received,
and they would begin to count all over again. In 1942, Heinrich
Himmler ordered that physical punishment in all of the German
concentration camps was to be administered by prisoners instead of
by the SS barracks leaders. This was not only a new cruelty to the
prisoners, but devilishly clever, for if now prisoners died from the
blows, the authorities could wash their hands like Pilate and say,
'They were beaten to death not by the SS but by their own companions.' Of course, the majority of the barracks elders refused to perform this penal work on their companions, but some were willing
to do it in order to win advantages for themselves. A special whip-
ping group was then formed from among the professional criminals
and antisocial people" (*Wie war das im KZ Dachau?*).

Sales Hess adds some details to the description of the twenty-five
double lashes: "They were given with a horse whip. One SS man
stood on the right and one on the left. The prisoner lay on the rack,
a table-like construction made especially for this punishment. His
legs were tied on below and his hands clamped on above. The clothing varied: sometimes underpants were allowed, at other times the
prisoner had to lie down naked. Both SS men beat the prisoner
with all their force. . . . If the prisoner miscounted, the whole show
started over, so that sometimes the twenty-five lashes became thirty
or forty. Blood poured out in streams. One SS man bragged that
blood began to flow already on his first blow. Often the bent tips of
the horse whips tore deep wounds into the flesh. Even the clergy
were not exempted from this mishandling" (ibid.).

Emil Kiesel from the Archdiocese of Freiburg, I think, had to
bear the worst punishments of all the German clergy. They found a
rosary on him when he was admitted to Dachau. He had to undress
immediately and stand stark naked in the snow. The SS men made
a hellish racket, danced around him, ridiculed him, boxed his ears,
and beat him wildly. An hour later, he came from the cold into the
bath; then followed the usual admittance procedure.

Another time, Kiesel was clamped to the rack because he secretly
heard the confessions of two companions; a camp spy had reported
it. Kiesel refused to talk when the barracks leader wanted to know

what the two confessed. Thereupon he was put in the dark cell for forty-two days. The SS man at first visited him almost every day, held his revolver under his nose, and said: "If you don't tell me now what the two confessed, I'll kill you!" After many days of this torture, Kiesel answered the SS man: "Pull the trigger, please, so that I will finally have peace!" Then the SS man laughed sarcastically and left with the remark: "You would like that, you priest pig! But I don't want to make a martyr of you!" From then on, he left Kiesel in peace, until his forty-two days were up (see the interview between Prof. Hugo Ott and Msgr. Kiesel, FDA 1970).

What all the prisoners in Dachau had to put up with! Clergymen and Jews had to slap one another. As punishment, bread thieves had to stand all day outside on the prison street, barefoot and bareheaded, with only a short shirt on—in pouring rain. Many SS men put the skulls of former prisoners on their desks; that was supposed to "toughen" them.

It was probably the worst time of all for the rest of the prisoners when they learned that ninety-two Russian officers were supposed to be shot. It was in May 1944. Through the grapevine, it became known what the SS intended. Then the "national camp committees" secretly called for a strike. The password was, no one will go to work! When, after the usual morning roll call, orders were given to depart for the places of work, no one moved. Silently the twenty thousand prisoners stood there. The camp leader asked the camp scribe what was wrong. He explained to him that the people were disturbed because they had heard, by way of rumor, of the imminent shooting of the Russians. Then once again, orders were given to go to work; again no one moved.

This solidarity of their fellow prisoners touched the ninety-two officers, who stood on the camp street, already set apart from the other 20,000 prisoners. They did not want to buy their life at the cost of endangering their 20,000 companions. So one of them, Lieutenant-Colonel Tarassov, called to the prisoners: "Comrades, march! We die as we have lived, fighting for Russia. Farewell, friends! March!" But they still did not want to go to work. Then the SS telephoned for two guard companies of seven hundred men. They arrived with machine guns and rifles, but even at that, no one on the parade grounds moved.

Once more, Tarassov stepped up and asked for permission to talk to the camp scribe, a prisoner. Only then did the scribe decide, although with a heavy heart, to give the orders to move.

The 20,000 prisoners had hardly left, when fifteen heavily armed SS came up, took twelve of the Russian officers along, and led them about six hundred meters to the crematorium. In the execution ditch, right next to the crematorium, they were "liquidated," one after another.

Then the fifteen SS men marched back to the parade grounds, took another twelve Russians, and so forth until the last one fell under their bullets. Ninety-two marched silently to their death, after refusing to have 20,000 suffer difficulties because of them. (J. Neuhäusler, *Wie war das im KZ Dachau?*)

Earlier, in February, thirty-one Russians had been "liquidated," as the SS used to say. At the beginning of September, another ninety Russian prisoners were shot.

Besides these cruelties to the concentration camp prisoners, the infamous selections (picking out prisoners for the invalid transport) took place in Dachau. As a rule, these were done publicly, on the parade grounds. Franz Weinmann from the Archdiocese of Freiburg tells how the "invalids" were selected:

"A glance of the camp doctor at their swollen legs or the rash on their body or their crippled form or their weak condition was enough to have them ranked as 'worthless life.' A sign of the hand to the left—to death; to the right—to life. . . . Like cattle for the slaughter, they were sorted out without pity, with cold decision and calculation. Almost all were destined for the invalids' transport, that is, for transport to another camp where there were gas chambers. . . . In cattle cars, packed together, starving and in despair, they went to a certain death" (FDA).

Once a thousand men left for the railroad station. It was a death column. "Staring silently and numbly, they dragged themselves through a monstrous row of armed SS guard posts. Because the number of invalids was not enough, all sorts of sick prisoners who happened to be in the hospital had been forcefully removed and placed in this invalid transport to fill up the number of one thousand. Confreres of ours (clergymen) who were orderlies saved many from death, but they could not save all. Those condemned to death—

a *massa damnata*—went by us. All victims of the mystery of evil" (Weinmann).

The SS doctors also proceeded rigorously and brutally. Albert Riesterer heard a hospital doctor say to a prison orderly: "I need three cadavers this afternoon at one o'clock for a dissection because several doctor friends are coming and I want to show them something." Since the hearse had gone to the crematorium early that morning, there were no cadavers in the hospital at that time. But at one o'clock in the afternoon, the doctor had his cadavers; three lives were quickly snuffed out in Dachau! (FDA 90/1970)

As Father Friedrich Seitz reported later in a sermon, there were two prisoners among the orderlies who were infamous because of their sadism and "human butchery." "They sent countless prisoners to their death with injections." Seitz, who was admitted to Dachau in the middle of 1940, became an orderly in the hospital at the end of 1942. Often he had to watch as prison orderlies became envious of patients because of their gold teeth; too often then these were the "cause of death"; some were murdered in order to get their gold teeth!

In addition to these atrocities, there were many medical experiments, which often ended in death. For example, the malaria experiments of Professor Klaus Schilling (the prisoners called him "Bloody Schilling"). Professor Schilling (University of Munich), who had free entrance to Dachau, sometimes had thirty or fifty prisoners picked out and sent to the hospital where they were injected with malaria germs. If the persons were still living after eight days, they were injected again.

Bruno Theek adds: "Thus from our barracks alone, twenty clergymen were picked out one morning; a few days later eighteen were dead. In the same way, hundreds were repeatedly injected with phlegmon agents. I remember how, one morning at roll call, thirty Italians were picked out and sent to the hospital. By that evening, all thirty were dead!" (Keller, *Kanzel and Kaschott*)

In the Dachau Documentation, the number of prisoners who had to endure malaria experiments is set at 1,200. By the way, Professor Schilling, who was also called "Dr. Anopheles," was brought to trial in 1946. He was condemned to death and hanged. He refused the assistance of a priest (E. Weiler, *Redemptoristen Gedenkblätter*, October 1981).

Another SS doctor, General Assault Commander Dr. Rascher, did experiments in Dachau for the Air Force: high and low pressure, high and low temperatures, hypothermia, and so on. Once during winter a clergyman had to lie a whole night naked and without blankets upon a table with the windows open. He fainted, but his heart continued to pump. He held out until morning, until Dr. Rascher came and was satisfied with the experiment. If his heart had stopped, there would have been one less prisoner, that's all.

The body temperature of various experimental patients (EP) was artificially reduced to 80.6 degrees Fahrenheit by means of water and ice. Dr. Rascher's assistants had to measure and record the patients' temperatures every ten minutes. Most of the curves ended with an X. In the margin was a note: "At this temperature the patient died." This is what Father Karl Schmidt, who had to photograph these curves, and Father Sales Hess testify.

Reading about these SS barbarities (which could be enlarged by many more examples) often makes one disgusted and causes one to shake one's head. A normal person can hardly believe what cruelties took place in the concentration camp. It was the same even with the prisoners themselves in Dachau: "Hundreds of times we said in camp: 'If later on, books are written about the concentration camps, most of the readers will not believe that something like this was possible in our days, and those who believe will not be able to grasp it fully because they themselves were not part of it'" (Gottfried Engels, GID).

One has to agree with the writer Ernst Wiechert, who was imprisoned temporarily in the Buchenwald concentration camp in 1938 and once thus characterized the Nazi regime and its methods: "Our people, as it were, had fallen through a sieve, and the chaff had gained mastery over the wheat. God's wind had become the devil's wind. Never was naked power more shamelessly embellished, the 'image of God' more deeply violated."

12

LETTERS FROM 1944

It must have been horrifying to the prisoners in the concentration camp to watch as their companions were beaten, put on the rack, hanged, trampled on, shot, or subjected to medical experiments. And they could not protest; they had to keep silent, to swallow their bitterness and rage. What remained for them was trust in a good and helping God, in the sense of the well-known words of Dietrich Bonhoeffer (1906–1945): "Wondrously sheltered by good powers, we wait confidently for what may come. God is with us in the evening and in the morning and most certainly in each new day."

Franz Weinmann writes: "We silently defied the violence. We quietly bore the injustice. Courage was needed for that. Obstinate rage and repressed indignation shone in some faces. Others' looks betrayed equanimity and quiet pity. . . . In our ranks, too, there were those who quietly prayed for the tormented and also for the tormenters. And that was, I believe, the greatest weapon which we defenseless ones had" (FDA 90/1970).

Father Engelmar was among those who made use of this weapon daily. In the face of the general misery, the satanic cruelties, and the beastly atrocities, he never lost faith in a good and just God. Father Engelmar was a man of much prayer. Untiringly he stormed heaven that God would end the suffering and grant the world peace.

There are only a few of Father Engelmar's letters preserved from 1944. His letters were either rejected by the camp censor or, as is more probable, they were lost in the frequent bomb raids on Munich. It can no longer be verified to what degree "illegal letters" were smuggled out of the concentration camp at this time. It would have been possible, but it is hardly to be presumed, because evidently contact with "Waldes Franz," the SS man in Dachau who came from Greifendorf, had been broken off.

Let us hear several short excerpts from the Dachau letters of 1944. On January 2, he writes: "My dear ones! New year greetings in the Lord! Looking back with gratitude on all the happy and painful things of the past year, let us look once again into the future with childlike trust. The more people in unreasonable defiance want to go their own ways and so run to destruction, the more fervently we want to beg God to turn to good all the damage caused and the harm done, and to bring peace among his quarreling children" (BAD).

The admonition to prayer expressed in these lines is also found in a letter of January 23, 1944: "This war is claiming many victims. May God also soon take the blindness from people and lead them back to the right path, to true love and harmony! Let that continue to be the prayer of all of us" (BAD).

In his next letter, Father Engelmar wrote: "Even if I cannot see all my dear ones face to face, I am close to them in spirit through the intervention of our Father in heaven. I often think that, if Christ, who came from heaven to lead the world back to the Father, lived the life of a worker in seclusion for thirty years, so he will also graciously accept our non-priestly activity [he was still working at the SS pay station—ed.] for his purposes" (BAD 8.2.44).

In the same letter, we read: "God grant that the present time of testing will soon end, or at least that it will not break people, but make them better. We usually think that suffering leads to God, but we see that very hard afflictions also break many tepid persons and that their divine intention is not recognized by some. Nothing, however, is impossible with God, so we want to continue to storm heaven that God may have mercy on the many who have strayed and are severely tested" (BAD).

Since the death of his mother, Father Engelmar wrote on March 5, he finds it easier to bear something hard. "That makes me believe that mother is already permitted to rest on the fatherly heart of God in heaven. She will also help you in all needs and, above all, that we too may happily reach our paternal home in heaven. Now when so much around us is falling into ruins, one comes to realize more and more that the only thing which is important is eternity and that we try, in unselfish love, to bring joy to God and, for His sake, to our fellow human beings. Oh, if we could only come to the aid of all the needy and severely afflicted! If I could only obtain this grace from God, how happy I would be to take upon myself every sacrifice with his help" (BAD).

The next letter is dated May 7, 1944. Here we find the following: "It is often shocking to see and hear how people we meet, in spite of the afflictions with which God knocks on the door of their heart and wants to waken them from spiritual sleep, remain hardened and blind and rather become more hardened and bitter. On the other hand, one sees again and again how, according to the teachings of our religion, all the puzzles and difficulties which cause others so much trouble are so beautifully solved and we receive so much comfort and joy, as St. Paul already said: I overflow with joy in all my affliction. If one could only communicate the joy in God to everyone or cause them to seek joy according to God's will, not to roll around in the dust and dirt of the earth! We want to continue to ask God to draw people to Himself and give them a sense of true happiness with Him. . . . Your Hubert far away" (BAD).

With the remark, "Sometimes the mail is impeded through outside influences and the like!" Father Engelmar begins his next letter. He is referring to the bombings, especially of Munich. Then he continues: "But God continues to grant me life so that I might come closer to Him and do penance for my sins and the sins of others. Oh, how little it is one can do in the face of people's terrible coldness and forgetfulness of God! There is, however, also gratifying religious openness, which delights the heart" (BAD 21.5.44).

In the same letter, he continues: "When a person is far from the bustle of the world and meets with people from all over, his view is broadened, and he notices how short and insignificant this life is in comparison with eternity, with the eternal happiness or unhappiness of a person, a piece of which each person carries in his heart already here on earth, depending on whether he is filled with the purposes of God or the devil. In the month of May, we too can gather around the throne of Our Heavenly Queen in order to greet her and present to her the intentions of the severely tested human race" (BAD).

In a letter written on June 11, Father Engelmar mentions that he finds it very painful that he has been a burden to his relatives for such a long time and has not been able to earn his own living. "But God does not let Himself be outdone in generosity. Whatever is given to Him out of love, He will give back in temporal and, above all, in imperishable, eternal goods. . . . Let us hope that we will soon see each other again. But we want to wait patiently until God in His wise providence lets a change of conditions take place" (BAD).

In July 1944, the delivery of mail and packages to the prisoners in Dachau became even more difficult; the attacks on Munich and environs continued to increase; many mail trains were burned. Father Engelmar asked his loved ones at home to send only food which could be kept for a long time because some packages took many weeks to reach him.

In his letter of August 13, he reminds his relatives of the anniversary of his First Mass "When I think of the fifth anniversary of my First Mass on the fifteenth of this month, I feel sad, but still I thank God for all the happy and painful things of this time, mindful of the song: The time will come when you will understand that all was a blessing! In a very special way, I will ask Maria's patroness in these days to reward her for all the good she has done for me. May God reward her for it" (BAD).

Now there follows a break of several months in the letters between Father Engelmar and his sister Maria-Huberta. The next letter (which we have) is from January 1945.

13

FORMER PRISONERS SPEAK UP

To round out the picture of life and death in the Dachau concentration camp, let priests and lay people who were formerly concentration camp prisoners speak in the following short reports, arranged in mosaic-like fashion, about very diverse topics and procedures, with varying evaluations and attitudes.

Not everything they report can be related or transferred to Father Engelmar; he did not directly experience everything they describe. But he somehow heard about nearly everything, if it happened during his time in Dachau. Most of it he "suffered" along with the victims because he knew about it; others told him about it.

The reports overlap in some areas. Some things are given varying nuances. The chronological order of the events is also not always possible to determine. Too many years, too many decades had passed before many of the eyewitnesses wrote or were interviewed about them. And yet, they all contribute valuable information to the overall concentration camp picture. Let us pass these short reports in review.

♦ ♦ ♦

"During the eleven years in which Dachau existed, 'only' 35,000 persons died there; it was really the 'best' of all the camps!" (GID) Ferdinand Maurath, priest of the Archdiocese of Freiburg, wrote this. He remarked about the causes of sickness in Dachau: "Whoever had worked until then with pen and paper in an office and now suddenly had to work twelve hours a day with pickaxe and shovel outside—and that on two liters of cabbage soup, 300 grams of bread, and a small amount of sugar, whether you were twenty or sixty years old—whoever had to slave in all kinds of weather while often soaked and perspiring, whoever could never change his clothes *had* to get sick. Getting sick was almost a necessary consequence of being a prisoner. Already in 1941, there were 1,500 seriously sick persons among the 7,000 prisoners in Dachau" (GID).

◆ ◆ ◆

To the newcomers among the clergy in Dachau, Father Richard Frasl, a priest of the Diocese of Sankt Pölten, Austria, used to say: "It is kind of hard in the beginning, but it gets better. If you are ordered to a work group after four weeks, you have survived the worst." Frasl sometimes encouraged his confreres, saying: "I do not let myself be outdone by anyone in brotherly love!" As volunteer orderly together with Father Engelmar, he went to the typhus victims toward the end of the war, caught the disease, and died from it. A martyr of brotherly love!

◆ ◆ ◆

Much concern and headache was caused for the concentration camp priests by the memory of those members of their communities who had turned them in to the Gestapo. As a rule, it was a harmless remark which was the prisoners' doom, for example, what happened to the Austrian priest Joseph Rohrmoser: "In September 1939, I paid a pastoral call to a sick man of my parish. The visit was very short. The Polish campaign was going on. The sick man asked me the latest news, and I expressed my displeasure with the war and prophesied a bad end to it. A woman who heard my remarks about the war reported me to the Gestapo in Linz" (GID).

◆ ◆ ◆

A day in Dachau, even a very ordinary one, was, as Hans Carls states, never without pain and suffering and anxiety for the individual: "Even when one was not suffering directly under the rage of the SS men, he asked himself despondently what all could happen to him, should he not take his cap off quickly enough when a guard met him, or if he should unintentionally break one of the innumerable strict regulations, or if his face should displease the sentry."

◆ ◆ ◆

"Father Lenz, who 'wanted to be all things to all men' in the camp and who helped immense numbers of prisoners wherever and whenever he could, was reported one day by a spy because he obtained some clothing for miserably clothed prisoners outside of the priests' barracks. He was sentenced to three weeks in the standing cell for that. This torture the Jesuit survived relatively well because many assisted him, including those prisoners who had to do duty in the standing cell; they deceived the SS. Later when typhus began to rage, Father Lenz was one of those who volunteered to help. Soon he was infected with the disease. 'He must be saved!' was the unanimous opinion of all the prisoners who knew the selfless Father Lenz. A serum was prepared for him from the blood of those prisoners who had survived the disease and he was inoculated with it. His rescue was a success" (Father Richard Schneider, letter to R. Schnabel).

♦ ♦ ♦

"One of the basic facts about the concentration camp world which should never be forgotten is the constant uncertainty one had about one's future. One never knew whether he would sleep in the evening in the same place he had left in the morning. Through an order from Berlin, one could end up as quickly as lightning in the dismal enclosure in front of the crematorium, in order to be shot in the neck or hanged on the gallows before being put in the oven" (E. Michelet, *Die Freiheitsstrasse*).

♦ ♦ ♦

"Really, of what must we still be afraid," Nico Rost (*Goethe in Dachau*) asks in his diary, "of getting out of this hell, of catching typhus and the continuous threat of death from the SS behind us? In my opinion, of one thing only: our own conscience."

Even non-believers—Rost calls himself an atheist—could not pass over this question without some effect. The crushing camp life presented the individual with questions which he could not avoid if he wanted to survive spiritually.

The question of meaning was also repeatedly asked, often in a self-torturing way. Rost quotes an aphorism of Georg Lichtenberg, who wrote a hundred and fifty years before Hitler's lackey executioners came along: "I would give anything to know exactly for whom those acts are done, of which it is publicly said that they were done for the Fatherland."

♦ ♦ ♦

"About 3,000 priests from Europe were in the Dachau concentration camp. More than 1,000 died there: one of every two Polish priests and one of every four German priests. When the camp chapel was opened in January 1941, there were about 1,000 priests in the camp. Only 400 of them were alive in January 1945. About 800 Polish priests died in Dachau from violence, starvation and epidemics. . . . The number of priests who died from experiments was small, but those who survived this kind of criminal activity of a Professor Schilling or a Dr. Rascher will suffer from the results for the rest of their lives" (R. Schneider, FDA).

♦ ♦ ♦

The Austrian priest Father Alfred Berchtold tells about the boundless despair of the prisoners' life in Dachau:

"The whole thing breathed an indescribable solitude and despair. A sharp east wind blew. The sky was foggy grey. Here in this desert, I should now remain for weeks, months, maybe years. The words of Dante should stand over the entrance: 'Whoever enters here, abandon all hope!' A loud noise reaches my ear and wakes me from my hopeless brooding. A street roller approaches, pulled by about twenty prisoners. The heavy roller moves but slowly. I shudder. In the twentieth century, people pull a street roller! Right and left of the prisoners an SS man with a club . . ." (GID).

Among the prisoners pulling the roller, Berchtold recognizes several prominent people: the former mayor of Vienna (Dr. Richard Schmitz), Prince von Hohenberg, as well as the Secretary of State Colonel Adam; and he asked himself secretly, "What will then be my work in Dachau, if ministers of state have to pull street rollers?"

♦ ♦ ♦

"To all those who were not there but who like to say that it could hardly have been as bad as the former prisoners of the concentration camps always describe it, I would like to state emphatically that it was much worse than books or pictures can show. For no pen or brush is able to portray the continual spiritual torture and the daily guerrilla warfare of the prisoners for their life against the always new mean tricks and cruelties of the SS guards as we had to experience them in years of long, grinding imprisonment, not only from morning until evening but even night to night" (B. Theek, ibid.).

♦ ♦ ♦

"The best clothing in the concentration camp is inurement, and we had all laid up a good quantity of it long ago," writes Jean Bernard (ibid.). In 1942, the Luxembourg priest had heard that three hundred Russian officers had been brought to Dachau. Hardly six weeks later, they were led out of the camp and never seen again. Says Bernard, "Then on the next day, three hundred Russian uniforms were disinfected by us and cut into strips in the clothing mill for the clothing collection."

♦ ♦ ♦

"If someone were to ask me today, 'Would you rather be in Dachau for one year or five years in the penitentiary?' I would prefer the penitentiary without a second thought. There you still have certain rights. In the concentration camp, however, you were the lowest scum" (L. Lazarus, *Sie flohen vor dem Hakenkreuz*, Reinbeck, 1981).

♦ ♦ ♦

At the beginning of the 1940's, there were fleas in Dachau. They hid in the prisoners' straw sacks. For a long time, scabies went around, "a disgusting skin disease which caused a continual biting itch and was most probably brought in from the East. At times, we had a scabies check every day. . . .

"Whoever was sent to the hospital for scabies was in great danger of being inscribed for an invalid transport, which meant death without fail (by gas). . . . These transports left at night between 1:00 and 3:00; the invalids were clothed only in shirt and pants. . . . A confrere, Hermann Scheipers, escaped this fate, although he was already on the list of death candidates. A friendly orderly or hospital scribe secretly crossed his name from the list. Scheipers understandably kept quiet about it. Then a couple of weeks after the transport, the relatives received the communication that prisoner So-and-So had died of pneumonia" (Hermann Dümig).

♦ ♦ ♦

In 1941, Barracks 26, 28 (and 30), where the clergy lived, were separated from the rest of the camp by a high fence and barbed wire. The pastors were not allowed to communicate with the camp inhabitants. "Nevertheless there was one place of frequent communication, when the air was clear, and that was on the side toward the crematorium. There confessions were often heard, Communion secretly given; there too charitable gifts were exchanged and greetings from home swapped" (Gottfried Engels, GID).

♦   ♦   ♦

Informative observations about the psychological disposition of the prisoners were made by the Vienna doctor and psychologist Viktor E. Frankl (*Trotzdem Ja zum Leben sagen*). Besides a kind of grim humor, something else develops among doomed men—and that was what all concentration camp prisoners without exception were—namely, curiosity. Curiosity whether one will survive. Whether one will get away with one's skull unfractured, and so forth. The drive toward the new, the desire to investigate, the wish to test oneself, according to Frankl, kept many a concentration camp prisoner alive. The despondent had less chance of ever coming out of this hell alive.

"We were curious," writes Frankl, "what all now would happen and what the results would be. The results, for example, of having to stand stark naked and still wet from the shower outside in the cold of late fall. And the curiosity succeeded by surprises in the following days, for example, the surprise that one does not catch a cold."

Frankl was also surprised that he could sleep well on the third bunk of a three-bunk wooden bed next to two snorers, that he could get along without a pillow, that his gums remained healthy, although he never brushed his teeth during the entire time in prison, that you could wear the same shirt for half a year. And repeatedly—as the Austrian psychologist, who survived the concentration camp, says—the sense of wonder, fascination, the desire for something new, but also a deep longing "to be alone with oneself and with one's own thoughts, the longing for a little solitude."

♦   ♦   ♦

The mostly young SS men who guarded the camp had to leave

the Church before joining Hitler's bodyguard; in fact, they had to declare their willingness to shoot their father and mother, if necessary. "Daily it was drummed into them that the prisoners were not human beings, but rejects of the people's community" (S. Hess, ibid.).

◆ ◆ ◆

In the summer of 1944, according to Ernst Wilm, about seven hundred French prisoners were sent to Dachau, one hundred to each railroad car in which fifty at most had room. They had been given bread and water for two days on the journey. The train, however, had been underway for ten to twelve days. Wilm writes: "When the cars were opened in Dachau, a terrible smell of dead bodies greeted the prisoners sent to unload the cars and the SS crew accompanying them. . . . Of the seven hundred prisoners, not four hundred were still alive. The others had probably suffocated or had killed themselves in the fight for air" (*Dachau*).

14

SECRET PASTORAL WORK AMONG RUSSIAN PRISONERS

After these eyewitness reports of former concentration camp prisoners, clergy and lay, let us return to Father Engelmar. We said Father Engelmar did not experience everything described in the accounts; not everything strung together there was known to him. But it was the milieu in which he had to live and suffer with his confreres.

We know from Father Engelmar that he did much for the Russian prisoners during the last years of his time in the concentration camp. This is attested to in numerous reports of former prisoners. The Russian prisoners, it is true, were influenced by the atheistic-Marxist regime of their land, but they had not become anti-religious; on the contrary, they were interested in everything religious.

Contact with the Russians began for Father Engelmar in the Messerschmitt Barracks of Dachau where, after his activity in the pay station, he worked with other German and Austrian clergy. Father Hans Brantzen writes: "When we clergy were dismissed from the pay station because of several 'incidents,' we [he means himself and Father Engelmar—ed.] found ourselves in the same detachment: the Messerschmitt airplane barracks with day and night shifts. We worked ourselves up to controllers and thereby procured the possibility of doing some good for the poor Russian young men and the small Frenchmen and Italians and, in fact, for all those who were under us" (FN).

The report says this about Father Engelmar: "Here in Messerschmitt, we experienced an unusual occurrence relating to Father

Engelmar which expressed in a special way his readiness to help those persons who were searching religiously. There a Russian, the father of a family, Peter by name, had to introduce us to the rudiments of technology. He was a good man, father of two children, who, with their mother, are most likely still waiting for him today. Peter revealed himself as a simple but profound and spiritually mature person who saw and tackled the problems of life. Often during the night shift at Messerschmitt, there were discussions about God: Nicodemus hours of a peculiar kind. Father Engelmar took more and more interest in this searching man. The two met often outside work time on the camp street for discussions. There developed a refined spiritual friendship between the two. In order to be able to communicate better with Peter, Father Engelmar diligently learned Russian. But Peter retained a last uncertainty and a last fear."

This report, written in 1950, contains still another reference to the Russian prisoner. After the death of Father Engelmar, he was so deeply touched that he decided to convert to the Catholic Church. Brantzen: "The decision to volunteer for the hospital barracks broke the ice for Peter and removed the last hindrance. The death of his missionary shook him terribly. He venerated Father Engelmar like a saint. He also sent a smuggled letter to his relatives in which he praised Father Unzeitig as a saint who had brought him Christ" (FN).

Similarly Father Josef Witthaut (Brügge, Westphalia) praises Father Engelmar. Witthaut was admitted to Dachau at the beginning of August 1944 and worked with Father Engelmar for several months. In a personal letter of September 1945 to Sister Adelhilde (Regina) Unzeitig (Witthaut was the hometown pastor of one of her fellow sisters), we find this about Father Engelmar: "He always seemed to think only of how he could help others. He always thought of himself last. When a package came from home, he always had acquaintances whom he had to help. Also many confreres also knew that Hubert Unzeitig always knew where there was hunger to be stilled. So quite a number of gifts passed through his hands to lay prisoners, many of whom he knew because of his long imprisonment and who then found help through him in the Priests' Barracks No. 26" (GA).

Secretly and very cautiously, Father Engelmar did his pastoral and charitable work in the camp. Many worked with him. In spite of continual threats of very severe punishment, the sacraments were administered to the laity and priests, the dying were assisted in the concentration camp. Often priests wrapped hosts in newspaper and secretly gave them to the prisoners.

In this the clergy received much help from outside. The pastor of the town of Dachau, Father Pfanzelt, for example, was a master at getting around the SS, finding laity to act as couriers, or organizing the women in his town when the mail could not deliver any more packages. Josefa Mack ("Mädi"), a candidate of the Poor School Sisters, inconspicuously brought hosts, Mass wine, candles, medicines, and other valuable things through the plantation. Without this help, the priest prisoners would not have been able to render many services, especially in the hospital.

Piety, steadfastness, and idealism distinguished most priests in Dachau. Besides the pastoral activity, there was a lively intellectual activity among the clergy, for example, the cultivation of music for the beautification of the liturgy or the meeting of theological work groups, despite strict prohibition. That contributed to making the desolation and hopelessness of camp life a little more bearable for the clergy.

The high point of the priests' camp life was the secret ordination to the priesthood of the deacon Karl Leisner by the imprisoned French bishop Gabriel Piguet from Clermont-Ferrand on the Third Sunday of Advent 1944. Maybe this was the most impressive ordination to the priesthood in all of church history, with hundreds of prisoner priests praying for the new priest. Father Engelmar was probably one of the clergy who laid his hands on the head of Karl Leisner in the Dachau camp chapel.

Father Engelmar also belonged to the priests who translated parts of Holy Scripture, passages out of the *Imitation of Christ*, and texts from the catechism into Russian. The "missionizing" of the Russian prisoners was, as we mentioned above, a special concern of his. These prisoners were either young men who had been deported from Russia "for sabotage" and had been put to work in German defense plants, or Russian civilians (among them many Ukrainians) who had come to Dachau from August 1942 on.

Hermann Dümig, who knew Father Engelmar from the time when they studied together in Würzburg, writes thus about him and his care for the Russian prisoners: "His pastoral zeal knew no limits. In the daily religious discussions, all the doubts and hesitations of a Russian prisoner, an engineer in civil life, disappeared, so that he promised to bring his civil marriage in order after his return and to practice the Christian faith again. . . . Later, that is, during that time so terrible for the prisoners just before liberation, Father Engelmar took over the job of group elder in order to be able to help the poor comrades pastorally" (MS/GA and mmm/Cologne).

Only later did it become known that the Russian engineer mentioned by Dümig was in fact a high Party official. On this Communist—his name was Sharashadev—Father Engelmar must have exercised an unusually profound influence.

It is universally attested that Father Engelmar took care of the Russian prisoners in an exemplary, self-sacrificing way. In the final analysis, much heroism took place here secretly, hidden underneath the loud bustle of camp life. For Father Engelmar, what the Carmelite Edith Stein (1891–1942) once formulated turned out to be absolutely true: "I knew from my first years of life that it is much more important to be good than smart."

15

VOLUNTEERING FOR THE TYPHUS BARRACKS

In the last weeks of December 1944 and in January 1945, the situation in Dachau got worse and worse: within a few weeks, a typhus epidemic had taken hold of the camp. The persons who had contracted typhus were packed together in certain barracks because the hospital could not hold them anymore.

Exposed to the disease without protection, the sick died like flies. Camp statistics show a daily average of more than one hundred deaths (see GID). One barracks with 1,600 men had only 400 after several weeks.

In the barracks, the conditions were dreadful. The sick lay delirious in their own filth, groaned, cried out, went crazy, and rolled in the throes of attacks. They were covered over and over with lice (the carriers of the disease!) and fleas and lay on bare boards.

Paul Ferrier describes the dreadful conditions in the Dachau typhus barracks like this: "We were full of lice and fleas. Many did not have a mattress anymore and lay on the bare boards. Since they could not get up, needs were taken care of on the spot. The excrement fell from the upper beds to the lower. If someone got too dirty, he was dragged to the wash room at the demand of his comrades, scrubbed off with rough brushes and thrown back on the boards" (quoted by J. Joos, *Leben auf Widerruf*). About the manner of disinfecting the patients (end of January 1945), Ferrier writes: "At 6 o'clock in the morning we had to go for a bath. Whoever could not walk was thrown on a cart naked or half naked. It was very cold. Many of us had 110 degree fever. Whoever did not walk fast enough was beaten by the barracks elder. In the shower, whoever did not succeed in getting to the spray immediately was dragged over the cement floor and dipped into a water container. . . . The return to the barracks took place in the evening at 8 o'clock, barefoot; many were without clothes. We were held, therefore, for fourteen hours in the bath without food or drink. . . . The number of deaths went up considerably in the following days. The bodies, with an identification tag around the ankle, were stacked up in the washroom in piles of ten alongside the barracks. From there, they were taken to the crematorium, after gold teeth and fillings had been removed."

According to Kupfer-Koberwitz (*Die Mächtigen und die Hilflosen*), 2,800 persons died in the camp just in January 1945, most of them of typhus.

Volunteers Wanted!

Because of the direct danger of death, hardly anyone was willing to serve as an orderly in the infected barracks. In this time of worst need and greatest danger, as typhus raged, as nurses and doctors died, the call came from the camp administration: Volunteers sought for the infected barracks! They turned especially to the priests.

Father Sales Hess writes: "In these straits, the camp administration remembered the clergy. All of a sudden, they recognized our spirit of sacrifice, although otherwise we were only parasites and leeches in the eyes of the SS. The decision was not easy; it required heroism of the highest order. Whoever signed up for volunteer orderly service in the infected barracks could not return anymore to his own barracks. Mass was out for him from then on. Over there with the poor invalids, lots of work, the most distasteful orderly service waited for him. In addition, there was the constant danger of infection and the lack of medical supplies. Under the circumstances, each volunteer could count on his own death with ninety percent certainty. How everyone looked forward to seeing his loved ones again at home, to returning to the long desired pastoral work! And yet, there were weighty grounds for accepting such orderly service. . . . No SS man came anymore into this lice-filled isolation. The orderlies could do pastoral work, since they could hardly do anything for the cure of the typhus patients" (ibid.).

Whatever the camp administration had in mind with this call, the priests took up the appeal of the SS. "There were ten volunteers from Barracks 26 and ten from Barracks 28, all helpers in the truest sense of the word. Zealots for the salvation of souls! Upon their entrance into the death barracks, a lively pastoral activity developed. Everyone who wanted could go to confession, receive Holy Communion, receive the Anointing of the Sick, and begin his last difficult journey calmly and with the comforts of the Church" (S. Hess).

Of the twenty priests who volunteered as orderlies, ten were German and ten were Polish. They had made the decision to offer their lives in the service of Christian love of neighbor, in the service of the poorest of the poor. "It was a heroic decision of heroic clerical Good Samaritans" (FDA). Among the twenty priests was also Father Engelmar.

Father Otto Pies remembers that the twenty priests volunteered "with full understanding of the danger and in readiness to offer their lives. . . . For many months, valuable groceries, fruit, and medicines were gathered daily in the priests' barracks and, in spite of the priests' own need and danger, put at the disposal of the sick in the hospital (and in the infected barracks) without respect to person or religion, and in spite of the order not to enter the hospital or help the sick. . . . Many priests also signed up to give blood to save the life of endangered comrades. Very little took place publicly; most remained hidden, and that was very much. In spite of orders to the contrary, priests went in and out of the hospital continually to care for the sick and give them the sacraments, and this also happened in the infected barracks. For those who know, it is certain that charity reached a more than average degree, yes, with not a few priests a heroic degree" (quoted by R. Schnabel, ibid.).

A Hard, Almost Superhuman Service

At the time when Father Engelmar and his confreres volunteered for orderly service with the typhus patients, the need was extremely great. Father Josef Witthaut, who was a friend of Father Engelmar, reports: "Every morning, the dead bodies, mercifully half-covered with snow, which waited to be transported away by the peat-bog express, were a gruesome proof of what was going on in the infested barracks. As bunk bed neighbor to Father Engelmar, I can say for sure that he was aware of the seriousness of his decision when he volunteered" (SvD 11/69).

According to Father Johannes Maria Lenz, the twenty priests volunteered for service in answer to an appeal by camp dean Georg Schelling, on February 11, 1945 (Quinquagesima Sunday). Probably, as several former prisoners have stated, Father Engelmar had "sneaked" into another barracks weeks before on his own. He had become barracks scribe for the Russian prisoners in order to be able to do pastoral work among them "more undisturbed," and also to care for the dying. Now, on February 11, Father Engelmar's service to the typhus victims became "official," so to speak.

That was a fateful decision, and a hard, almost inhuman, service! "As always, the priests were forbidden under threat of serious punishment to do any religious work in the camp. But they did not pay any attention to the order. They were priests, and here there were souls at stake, the souls of those condemned to a ghastly death. . . . As they went into the death zone, they knew they were on a death mission. Eighteen of the twenty volunteer clerical orderlies fell victim to the epidemic. Only two survived: the Dominican Father Leonhard Roth and the Jesuit Johannes Maria Lenz" (A. Berger, *Kreuz hinter Stacheldraht*).

The picture which presented itself to the volunteer orderlies was an inferno more horrible than Dante could have depicted. It was hell, not to be described in words. Yet the twenty priests understood that the appeal made to them was God's will. They went to work: they "swept the boards and plank-beds as clean as they could, washed the filthy, sweating, stinking, emaciated bodies, collected the lice-infested clothes and burned them. The fire ate its way into the pile of clothes crawling with lice and destroyed the clothes, but the vermin seemed to be immortal. . . . And continuously new transports of prisoners from the East rolled into camp, and every transport brought new legions of vermin along" (A. Berger, ibid.).

Further details of the service of the twenty volunteer orderlies are supplied in quantity by Father Johannes Maria Lenz (ibid.). During his Good Samaritan service in the typhus barracks, he crawled from bed to bed—with the Holy Eucharist in a butter carton—prayed with the dying, administered the Sacraments and crawled to the next person. Lenz writes:

"Through the indescribable filth of camp poverty, through contagion, lice and hunger, the Lord accompanied us—through typhus, diarrhea, enterocolitis (inflammation of the small and large intestine), and scabies; the medics talked of cholera. . . . The ban on pastoral work also held for the typhus barracks, but the fear of death kept the SS away. . . . The beds, three high, were frighteningly poor; they should have been simple wooden frames with straw mattresses, but now they had only wood planks. They were covered with dirt and lice, pus, spit, and excrement . . . Often even the planks were missing. Other prisoners had taken them to cook potatoes or heat the barracks. The window panes were missing. An ice cold wind blew pitilessly on the dying. . . . One night at 11:30, we were wakened by a blood-curdling scream. A sick man climbed from his bed with his hand bleeding. What had happened? Well, he had tied his few belongings to his wrist with a string. Now a rapacious companion in suffering from the far away Altai Mountains had come to rob him. Awakened by a pull on the string, the sick man had drawn his belongings to himself; but then a sharp knife passed over the string and his hand. . . . Whenever my hands were dirty, I went from the sleeping quarters of the barracks to the living room. There in the living area stood two bowls of lysol solution. After washing my hands in them, I went back. Four or five times a day, I searched my underwear for lice. My daily find was thirty to fifty lice."

Modesty was His Nature

Thanks to Father Lenz, we have very detailed descriptions of the work of the twenty priests for the typhus patients. He writes amply about Father Engelmar and his quiet and heroic work with the sick. Much information and many thoughts are found in a personal letter which he wrote to Sister Adelhilde Unzeitig in 1947 (two years after the end of the War) and which is printed in his book about Dachau.

In this letter, Father Lenz calls Hubert Unzeitig his friend: "In him, I really had an especially zealous collaborator in all charitable undertakings. Our Father Engelmar was a quiet, selfless helper, a genuinely priestly victim soul. . . . Modesty was his nature. He could be very energetic, however, as soon as the truth, objective grounds, were at stake. He was never interested in pushing himself forward, and he never lost his calm, even when standing up ruthlessly for the truth. Such selflessness does not know any injury to love, even in reproof."

Father Engelmar's main interest, according to Father Lenz, was pastoral work with the sick and dying concentration camp prisoners. "The corporal assistance which he gave was only the necessary condition and fruit of his priestly love of neighbor. He gladly heard the confessions of his poor ones and in his quiet, kind way comforted them in the misery of the camp. . . . Hubert was a man who did not shun any sacrifice. But the most valuable thing about him was his supernatural, priestly attitude of soul." And he continues: "Father Engelmar sacrificed all of his free time for the poor comrades of various nations. He gave them much more than his time and selfless care; he gave them his whole priestly love. That was his goal, while death took a terrible toll."

The letter goes on: "One day, I was called to the window of the second room. Our Hubert had knocked and asked for me. I do not remember anymore what he wanted. But he was cheerful, in spite of the deadly earnestness of the situation. The happiness of his priestly activity shone in his noble, finely etched features. Several days later, he once again had me called to the window at noon. He wanted Oil of the Sick for his dying patients; his had run out. Luckily I could help him out a little. But his face frightened me this time. His eyes glowed with high fever and his sunken cheeks showed sharply edged red spots. Slightly bent, he stood there. He held his thin prison jacket pulled up tight because he was shaking with fever chills. It was still winter, about February 20, 1945. He answered my warning about caution with a friendly smile. He completely underestimated his dangerous condition and seemed not to realize that death already held him irrevocably in its hand. He still wanted to help many people and many waited for his help. About himself, however, he did not think."

So far Father Lenz. This Jesuit was one of the most active priests in the Dachau concentration camp, but also one of the most ill-treated: "For six and a half years, I was in prison, five of them in Dachau, three times in the penalty company, twelve days and nights in the standing cell, two times close to death from typhus—and how many times from starvation! In danger of death from work, beatings, the gun. Robbed of six and a half years of life—of the best years of life. A misfortune? In no way! It was the will of God, and God wants only the good."

The last sentence Father Engelmar could also have written. He, too, put all he did in the hands of God. His union with God was so great that he bore all suffering bravely and courageously, that his love of his fellow prisoners knew no limits. Out of his attention to God grew his attention to men. He acted completely in accord with the words of Helder Camara: "If you have a piece of wood you can throw in the water, be yourself a piece of living wood for the shipwrecked, your brothers!"

"Love Doubles One's Strength"

Father Engelmar still wrote a few letters in the last weeks of his life. Their delivery had become difficult because of the increased bombing raids toward the end of the war. In a letter of January 14, 1945, he thanks Father Otto Heberling for the Christmas mail and the packages received. In closing, he says: "With trust in the Lord, we go into the new year and hope to be able to work again for the glory of God and the salvation of souls. Most cordial greetings to all confreres, your grateful H. Unzeitig" (BAD).

In his next letter, dated January 28, 1945, Father Engelmar likewise heartily thanks his sister for all the valuable charitable gifts received. He hopes that God will soon give peace to mankind, and he writes toward the end of the letter: "For the rest, let us continue to accept from the hand of God what He will send us in the future and offer everything up to Him, with the request that He may very soon grant to the severely tried human race the peace it so ardently longs for."

In his last letter from Dachau—without date and address but probably written to Sister Adelhilde—Father Engelmar's overpowering love for God and man shines forth once more. Probably he was already sick when he wrote these lines, but did not want to let his relatives know. Someone wrote on the original of this letter, "Sister Adelhilde Unzeitig, Neuenbeken." Further, "The last letter of Father Engelmar Unzeitig, C.M.M. from the concentration camp." This letter is, so to say, Father Engelmar's last will, his "testament." Here it is unabridged:

My dear sister,

I also was very happy to receive a sign of life from you after a long time. Maybe the disturbed transportation conditions are also at fault. All that, however, does not deprive us of our composure, since we feel ourselves well protected in the hand of God, as St. Paul says: Whether we live or die, we are the Lord's! All we do, will, and can, what is it but His grace which carries and leads us? His almighty grace helps us over the difficulties; yes, as St. Felicity said, the Lord Himself suffers in us and struggles together with our good will for the triumph of His grace. So, we can increase His glory, if we do not put any hindrance in the way of His grace and surrender ourselves totally to His will. Love doubles one's strength, makes one inventive, renders one interiorly free and happy. It has really not entered into the heart of any man what God has prepared for those who love Him. Of course, they too are buffeted by the rough reality of this world with all its haste and chase and tumultuous wishes and demands, with its dissension and hate like a biting frost, but the rays of the warming sun of the love of the all-good Father are stronger and will triumph, the Good is undying and victory must remain with God, even if it sometimes seems useless for us to spread love in the world. Nevertheless, one sees again and again that the human heart is attuned to love, and it cannot withstand its power in the long run, if it is truly based on God and not on creatures. We want to continue to do and offer everything so that love and peace may soon reign again.

Has Friedrich not written you for such a long time? May God strengthen and protect and comfort him. We are, thank God, still well and intact, including Father Lenz. Always thinking of you in prayer, I greet you most cordially. Your Hubert. (BAD, February 1945)

A few weeks, maybe only a few days, after this letter, Father Engelmar died, on March 2, 1945, only one day after his birthday. He was thirty-four years old; perhaps we should say thirty-four years young! The death certificate (the original, as well as his original file card from the Dachau concentration camp, is to be found at the

International Red Cross Search Service in Arolsen, Germany) has the following data:

"Departure through death!" stands in bold letters at the top of the certificate, which was made out on March 2, 1945, in the "Prisoners' Hospital Building" of the concentration camp. Then follow personal data: birth date, place of birth, profession, religion, referring office (Stapo Linz 667/41 IID), date of hospital entry: February 20, 1945, and the hour of death: 0720 hours. Furthermore, post-mortem examination: March 2, 1945, at 1400 hours. Diagnosis: typhus exanthemata." Then the signature (unreadable!) of the camp doctor, SS Captain of Company Commanders. The hour of death is also known: Father Engelmar died on Friday, March 2, 1945, at 7:20 AM. A few more details about the last days of his sickness we learn from a letter of Father Joseph Witthaut to Sr. Adelhilde, dated September 21, 1945:

"Hubert's barracks became especially endangered (by typhus) and was put in strict isolation, and after several days it was said that Hubert had also caught the disease and had been sent to the hospital. [His entrance in the hospital, as we know from the death certificate mentioned above, took place on February 20, 1945.—ed.] Then we helped continually from the priests' barracks. I believe that he also had good care. At least, we had contact with him continually through several good orderlies, who constantly kept us up to date on the condition of the sick priests. It was said that Hubert Unzeitig was on the way to recovery and had survived the crisis. Then came a relapse; the community [the Dachau priests—ed.] prayed for him especially for two days, but then came the notice of his death anyway. After having been administered the Last Sacraments, he made his way to the Lord. His body then, together with another priest, was reverently laid out and blessed. The whole community then said the Office for a Dead Priest and offered up a solemn Requiem for him" (GA).

16

A HERO OF CHARITY

Father Engelmar's death was the death of a martyr, of a man who, as it were, quietly overlooked his own person and only cared about others; who never made much of himself; who did not complain, but suffered and kept silence; who found comfort in the thought of Christ who was mocked and ridiculed on the cross; who showed calmness and composure in dangerous, often desperate moments; who gave such a heroic example that even the most discouraged could take courage again. His body was burned in the Dachau crematorium, all by itself, which was due to an initiative of Father Richard Schneider.

Schneider, born in 1893, had been in Dachau since November 1940. He knew Father Engelmar very well, lived with him in Room 2 of the Priests' Barracks and appreciated his quiet, unobtrusive and modest ways. In a personal letter, he admits: "I, like all my confreres, saw a saint in Father Engelmar. Because I appreciated him so much, I tried at that time to get his ashes" (GA).

That was a risky undertaking; it could have cost the heads of Schneider and all others involved. But this clergyman from Hundheim near Tauberbischofsheim had worked out a plan. He writes: "After the announcement of his death, my one thought was, how would it be possible to get his mortal remains, which otherwise would be put in an ash grave with many others after being burned in the crematorium? My connections with the head of the crematorium [a criminal from Karlsruhe by the name of Mahl—ed.] made it possible. I asked him whether he could burn the body of Unzeitig by itself during the night when he worked there alone and bring me the ashes. He told me to bring him his (Unzeitig's) camp number. This number was written with ink on the arm or stomach of every body. This was necessary because it was recorded in the camp files whether a prisoner had gold fillings, and these were removed according to this number before the body was brought to the crematorium on a wagon. In fact, before we left for work one morning, the head of the crematorium brought me the ashes in a bag. When they asked him at the camp entrance what he had in the bag, he said, "Blotting sand," and was allowed to go on. . . . I sewed the ashes in a small bag, upon which I wrote with India ink: *Vera cinera* [correct: *veri cineres*—ed.] *beati in Domino defuncti P. Unzeitig*, then closed them in a small box, upon which was carved a U, and had them brought out of the plantation to the city of Dachau by Mr. Leo Pfanzer" (GA).

Leo Pfanzer, born in 1903 in Höchberg near Würzburg, was vice president of Baywa (a farmers' supply company) in Dachau. Because he frequently had business contacts with the concentration camp plantation (potato shipments, purchase of flowers, sale of seeds, and the like), it did not attract attention when he talked briefly with one or the other prisoner. Pfanzer was a member of the party and therefore, for the SS people, above suspicion. Still he was anything but a supporter of the National Socialists. The clergymen could count on him a hundred percent.

Pfanzer, then, received Father Engelmar's ashes in the concentration camp. According to him, there were small pieces of bone as well as teeth in the little box handed over by Father Schneider. At first, he kept everything in his home in Dachau and then brought it to Würzburg by train at the end of March 1945. In a conversation at his home in Plattling near Straubing in September 1981, Leo Pfanzer said:

"I wanted to hand over the ashes myself; the Nazi regime was still in existence and you had to be careful. And I wanted to see my beloved Würzburg, which had been bombed in the meantime, to look around for my relatives and acquaintances. So I took the opportunity to visit the Franconian metropolis, which now lay in ruin and ashes. In the house of the Mariannhill Missionaries on Mönchsberg—surprisingly it had survived the bombing—I handed over the ashes to the priests there. With that, I had done all I was commissioned to do."

What happened after that we learn from a letter of Father Willehad Krause, Rector of Pius Seminary in Würzburg, which he wrote to the Unzeitig sisters on July 7, 1947:

"Often I think of his [Father Engelmar's—ed.] First Mass and I am still happy that I could be there and preach for him. Do you know that we have buried his ashes in our grave here in the cemetery? There was a terrible confusion here at the time. On March 16, 1945, Würzburg was nearly totally destroyed by a single bombing raid. Nothing was left of the inner city. Since our seminary is on the outskirts of the city, we escaped with only some damage. On March 29, I received in a very roundabout way a small wooden box. Inside it were the ashes of our Father Engelmar in a small linen bag. An accompanying note said that they were the genuine ashes. On March 30, Good Friday, we lowered this small box into our vault, while the incendiary bombs were still exploding in the cemetery. Several weeks ago [that is, in June 1947—ed.], I obtained permission from the cemetery authorities to open the vault and put the ashes in a brass urn, which had been obtained in the meantime. The small linen bag had decayed. On the bottom of the small box, we found two letters in an envelope. But they were so stuck together from the moisture that we could not completely save them anymore. The one letter was written with a pencil. I am guessing that you, Miss Marie, were the sender. The other sheet was written with a typewriter, but could no longer be deciphered. Then we neatly soldered up the urn and lowered it again into our vault. Now at least, he can rest among his confreres here in Würzburg, where he studied and received Holy Orders. I am convinced that he is our intercessor in Heaven. In the last battles for Würzburg in April 1945, when we lay in the line of artillery fire and the shells were falling on the house and church, I repeatedly called on Father Engelmar, and I am convinced that we owe it to his intercession that we came through the disaster so well. Cordial greetings to all. Yours sincerely in Christ, Father Willehad Krause, Rector" (GA).

The Last Weeks in Dachau

This biography could simply end with the death of Father Engelmar and the burial of his ashes in the cemetery in Würzburg. But the Dachau concentration camp lasted several weeks longer.

Therefore we want to remain here a little, before we return once again briefly to Father Engelmar.

In the last weeks before the end of the war, wild rumors circulated in the camp. Once it was said that the SS had received the order from Berlin to blow up the whole camp, once there was talk of a bombing raid by the German Air Force, then again of a command by Heinrich Himmler to "finish off" all the camp inhabitants by shooting them.

In the midst of this coming and going of rumors and excitement, almost out of the blue a number of clergymen were released at the end of March. It began on Tuesday of Holy Week, March 27, 1945. On the certificate of release was written: "Released by order of the Reich's Office of Security on March 23, 1945." Great relief in the camp! Hope came to life again and took hold also of the prisoners of the other barracks.

The release of the clergymen took place on the basis of four lists which barracks scribe and camp dean Georg Schelling had had to prepare weeks before, on February 15. On that date, there were 1,478 clergymen in the camp. Father Engelmar's name was also on the list; he would have been (most probably) among the clergymen released "early" if . . . Yes, if he had still been alive! One former prisoner asserted that Unzeitig's name was even called out. The list made in the middle of February 1945 had not been brought up to date; it was not known who of the persons on the list had already died. The general confusion in the camp was that great!

The releases went on from March 27 to April 11. The clergymen had to sign a statement before their release that they had not contracted any disease in the camp, that they did not make any claims on the camp, and that they would keep silent about what went on in the camp. They were given some provisions for the journey and a few coins, and released. From about 320 clergymen from Germany, Austria, and the German-speaking parts of Czechoslovakia, 168 received their freedom.

And why this release of prisoners? According to one prisoner, Hitler wanted Pope Pius XII to negotiate with the Allies for a possible common campaign against the Communist East. At that, the pope was supposed to have demanded that, before he would consider any mediation, all priests had to be released from the concentration camps. That is the explanation for the short "wave of releases" in March-April 1945. Then Himmler stopped further releases when it became clear that the Allies would not agree at all to Hitler's proposals. The remaining clergymen, therefore, had to stay in Dachau with about 30,000 other prisoners until the order was given for the infamous "death march" at the end of April.

On April 26, 1945, all prisoners from the German Reich, as well as part of the Russians and Yugoslavians, all told about 7,000 men, were called to the parade grounds. Each was given a wool blanket and two days' provisions. Then the column had to move out: an evacuation march in the direction of the Otztal Alps! The remaining prisoners (about 20,000 to 24,000) were supposed to be killed "in due time."

How many of the "evacuated" survived the death march, which ended in Waakirchen on Tegernsee on May 1, 1945, is not known. Of the 89 clergymen who took part in the march, 35 were freed in an escape at night led by the Jesuit priest Father Otto Pies; some were able to escape on their own. The rest of the clergymen on the march were allowed to "intern" themselves in a nearby cemetery of a southern Bavarian pastor; they convinced their guards that it was useless to march on, since the front was drawing ever closer; they should let them go.

For the prisoners remaining in Dachau, the promised day came on April 29, 1945. The Czech priest (barracks elder) Joseph Plojhar said at the liturgy: "I announce to you a great joy. The SS has left the camp; a white flag is flying from the main tower of the camp. Maintain discipline! Caution is imperative; a small number of SS (Combat Group Wicker) is still on the towers at the machine guns."

An SS squad with artillery lay near Schleissheim. It was supposed to fire on the camp but, because of the swift advance of the American tanks, never got to it. What now took place was wild chaos and joyful frenzy among the prisoners.

Hans Carls, quoting a Bavarian newspaper, says that the Americans entered the camp in the vicinity of the crematorium. "They immediately stormed the SS barracks and killed the SS men who resisted wherever they appeared . . . 'I never saw my men in such a mood before,' an American lieutenant said later. 'They were enraged, they ran down the camp street without care for cover. No one thought of his own life, after he had seen the starved prisoners in the railroad cars on the siding near the camp.' The happy prisoners screamed hysterically for joy when they saw the Americans. . . . When the short, hard fight was over, the dead from the SS garrison lay in grotesque positions next to the bodies of the prisoners who had had to die by the hundreds every day. The Americans suffered no losses" (ibid.).

The Austrian priest Johann Steinbock (*Das Ende von Dachau*) has probably described most fully the arrival of the Americans in the Dachau concentration camp. When the prisoners saw three American reconnaissance cars in front of the Jourhaus gate, they broke out in loud cheers. A Pole rushed through the gate toward the Americans, who were getting ready to ride in. A shot rang out and the Pole, wounded, had to be dragged to the hospital. At the entrance, the Americans were lifted to the shoulders of the prisoners and carried into the camp. One soldier took off his helmet—it was a woman, a reporter. During all the commotion on the parade grounds and in the SS buildings, an American soldier motioned for silence from up on the gallery of the Jourhaus. Then followed one of the most moving scenes of the day of liberation. The crowd grew silent and looked up at the soldier. He greeted them in German and wished them good luck on their liberation. Then he said: "Still, God is good. Although so many horrors have happened here, he grants us this day today, and this hour of liberation. Therefore, let us pray." And he took off his helmet, folded his hands and spoke with loud voice: "Almighty God, we thank you for the victory and the protection which you have given us." And he stood there for a time in silence, with bowed head.

"Still, God is good." The prisoners repeated the words of the American soldier in a whisper on the parade grounds of Dachau, where many of them had been enslaved for years by godless jailers and their helpers.

Buried in a Holy Place

After this description of the last weeks in the Dachau concentration camp—which is brief only because of lack of space—let us return again to Father Engelmar. In the autumn of 1968, a simple commemorative resting place was created for him in Sacred Heart Church of the Mariannhill Missionaries in Würzburg. His ashes were brought there on the afternoon of November 20, 1968 (Penance and Prayer Day, a national holiday in Germany). Besides many faithful, there were, above all, former concentration camp priests and many Mariannhill Missionaries.

The commemorative liturgy, festively prepared, had as a motto, "There is no greater love than this: to lay down one's life for one's friends" (Jn 15:13). The Rev. Dr. Sales Hess, O.S.B., gave the homily. In it, he described Father Engelmar as a person who, with an almost superhuman love and kindness, consumed himself in the service of his sick and dying fellow prisoners and finally gave his own life for them. Here are a couple of paragraphs from the homily:

"In this sermon, we don't want to make accusations against anything which has long been judged and condemned. We also do not want to canonize anyone. That is the duty of the Church. But justice demands that we priests from Dachau give witness to a heroism which surpassed the ordinary human level, and Father Engelmar deserves that we honor his heroism with today's celebration and lay his ashes to rest in a holy place. Father Engelmar was not just one of the nearly 3,000 clergymen of Dachau who, in a godless world, gave their life for Christ; Father Engelmar was a hero of charity, a hero of apostolic zeal. . . . For years he cared for the invalids with particular zeal, comforted them, heard their confessions, supplied them with groceries. . . . Father Engelmar climbed the heights of charity and priestly zeal in the last months of our imprisonment. . . . The sick rooms were filled with an unbearable smell of the epidemic. These caverns of death filled with filth and lice were his daily field of action. The space over the beds was so low that you could not even sit up. The priest, hunched over and on his knees, had to crawl from patient to patient. The patient's chest served as the sick table. . . . Most received the Last Sacraments, and no one who wanted the sacraments died without them, thanks to Father Engelmar and his assistants, something unbelievable for the hell of Dachau! . . . We may call out the words of Father Engelmar to today's Christians: Do good, for the good is immortal, and victory must remain with God!" (FN/GA)

So now the urn of ashes of Father Engelmar, this martyr of brotherly love, rests in the church where he was ordained in 1939. Already on November 20, 1968, after the transfer of the ashes, a

clergyman rightly said: "We should no longer pray *for* Father Engelmar, but *to* him."

In Father Engelmar, we have before us a man who led a truly
heroic life. He was a man whose path to the peak of perfection
led through the deep valley of humility and debasement. He was a
"concentrated" personality, that is, a personality which lived out of
the power of the religious, which radiated a spiritual power whose
origin cannot be explained by reason alone. In short, he was and is
a saint whose protection and intercession we can seek—in prayer.

17

TRACES OF LOVE

A number of individual statements by former concentration camp priests who knew Father Engelmar well will bring this biography to an end. They are either oral communications given in part at the Concentration Camp Priests' Meeting in Freiburg in September 1981, or declarations contained in the many letters written to the Mariannhill Missionaries (1981–84). All this most recent information shows again that Father Engelmar is not forgotten; he left traces behind, traces of love.

♦ ♦ ♦

Father Clemente Pereira, S.J.: "In the priests' barracks, I had my place directly behind Father Engelmar. It is somehow strange that I still have only him before my eyes now. At that time, I had the impression of a simple, modest, and deeply religious priest who did not talk much but, instead, certainly prayed much. . . . He was a saint! Without a doubt. I do not use this word lightly. But in Father Engelmar's case it fits; he was a holy priest!"

♦ ♦ ♦

Father Franz Schobesberger: "In Dachau, I had Father Engelmar as my neighbor at table. I can witness to his kindness and honest friendliness, especially his helpfulness, when he gladly gave me, the inexperienced newcomer in the concentration camp, without my asking for it, pieces of advice which proved very useful" (1982).

♦ ♦ ♦

Father Eugen Weiler: "His genuine priestly form stands very alive before my eyes; I would be very happy if Father Engelmar Hubert Unzeitig were raised to the honors of the altar, for the *advocatus diaboli* would most probably hardly be able to produce anything against him" (1981).

◆ ◆ ◆

Father Hermann Scheipers (East Germany): "Without words and without great gestures, Father Engelmar radiated something holy. He was undoubtedly one of the most inconspicuous and lovable confreres in Dachau. I knew him well. But he was so modest that there is almost nothing to say about him" (1981).

Two years later, Father Scheipers wrote: "Father Engelmar Unzeitig offered a wonderfully pure life's sacrifice in the following of Christ (at the beginning of 1945). . . . He died shortly before the liberation of the camp. He can certainly be put in the same line with Father Maximilian Kolbe, who sacrificed his life in the starvation cell at Auschwitz for the father of a family" ("Meine Erlebnisse im KZ Dachau," MS of 26.5.1983).

In January 1984, Father Scheipers, who was now living in Münster-Amelsbüren, added to his remarks: "In spite of the many faces which you saw daily then in the mass of priest prisoners, there were certain ones which you didn't forget. One of them was Father Engelmar's face. He impressed me from the beginning, for he radiated simplicity, humility, and modesty, as well as a continual inner happiness. When I heard—only after my liberation—of his offering of his life, I immediately thought: that fits him exactly! And I felt ashamed before him and also the others who had been carried off that I was still alive. . . . Perhaps I should have, after all, decided as Father Engelmar did: simply, happily, and full of trust! In any case, it would have been easier for me to reach the perfection which is the goal of us all" (letter to the editor, January 5, 1984).

Monsignor Josef Albinger: "Deep friendship bound me to Father Engelmar. We worked together in the Dachau Messerschmitt factory. There was a night shift and a day shift; every two weeks the shift was changed. Parts of the infamous V1 and V2 were also produced there. In this work, Father Engelmar was a picture of calmness, calmness and stability in all the terrible commotion of the concentration camp. He was recollected, friendly, composed" (1982).

◆ ◆ ◆

Father Heinz Römer: "In my opinion, this martyr of brotherly love also deserved to be raised to the honors of the altar" (1982).

◆ ◆ ◆

Monsignor Emil Kiesel: "Father Engelmar Unzeitig? He was a very dear, precious person. Love in person. More I cannot say. That he was: love!" (1982)

◆ ◆ ◆

The last sentence sums up all the statements about Father Engelmar best of all: "That he was: love!" Father Engelmar forgot his own life in heroic service for others, in love turned toward the helpless. In this point, he has very much similarity to the French missionary Charles de Foucauld (1858–1916), who once said: "Love, that means to exchange all well-being for all pains, for the sake of the Lord."

Father Engelmar was a simple man without a famous past, without special connections. He was an inconspicuous personality, very modest, almost shy. But love made him greater than the greatest of his time, that love about which we read in the first letter of John, "The commandment we have from him is this: whoever loves God must also love his brother" (1 Jn 4:21).

At no time in his life did Father Engelmar make a fuss about himself. On the contrary, he shunned everything which might have brought him attention and esteem. He spent himself in the service of God and man. He had no other pride than to be what he was without limit or condition: priest and religious. That was his greatness!

EPILOGUE

"The world is unbelieving not only out of evil,
but also out of disappointment at the tepidity
of Christians. The world is waiting for the
witness of our love."

Bishop Albert Stohr, Mainz

Father Engelmar Unzeitig was just one of many, one of thousands, who deserve to be presented to posterity in a detailed biography. The Mariannhill Missionary stands as a representative for all those who suffered unspeakably in Dachau and other camps, who were treated as non-persons, even as parasites, who had to experience so much hate and contempt in body and soul that it could not have been more terrible and cruel.

This book wants to be an act of reverence to the dead of Hitler's concentration camps and a sign of respect to those who survived Dachau and the other concentration camps. In addition, it would like to point out that we must learn from history; still more, that what once happened in Dachau and elsewhere must never happen again.

That is by no means to be taken for granted. For "even since May 8, 1945, the firebrand of war has not been extinguished in the world; there is torture and terrorism, violence and slavery. Inhuman misery to an unimaginable degree still exists" (Spiritual Word of the German Bishops' Conference, May 8, 1985, No. 7). What causes this? In other words, what caused war, horror, and slavery in the time of National Socialism? Because the order of things was wrong. God was pushed aside. People, race, the state took His place.

There is not a great danger among us today that we will put our people, our race, and the state in the place of God, but other things can be put in his place: material prosperity, consumerism, ideologies. The Jesuit priest from Munich, Father Alfred Delp (1907–1945), who himself became a victim of National Socialism, tells us what is crucial: "Bread is important, freedom is more important, but what is most important is unbroken loyalty and unbetrayed adoration."

That is essential, and everything else depends on it: adore God, bend the knee before Him, before Him alone. Man is never so great as when he goes on his knees before God. "We are completely free only when God alone governs," says Saint Augustine, the greatest of the Latin Church Fathers. We must give God the place in our lives which He deserves. That is true for the individual, and it is also true for human society. The greatest danger for the human person is godlessness, which is becoming widespread among humans in the form of forgetfulness of God.

To give God the first place, fulfill His will, keep His commandments, bend our knee before Him in adoration—that is the testament of the confessors and martyrs of Dachau, and also of Father Engelmar Unzeitig. We should keep it alive, for "Love of God is the source of the right love of neighbor" (Maximilian Kolbe).

A FINAL WORD FROM THE TRANSLATOR

A few lines are added here to bring the readers up to date on the Church process for the beatification and canonization of Father Engelmar.

The 1990 General Chapter of the Mariannhill Missionaries, the congregation to which Father Engelmar belonged, requested the Superior General of the congregation and his council to initiate the beatification process of Father Engelmar.

On March 16, 1991, the Superior General and his council appointed Father Wolfgang Zürrlein as Postulator for the beatification process and Father Adalbert Balling as Vice Postulator. At the same time, they officially petitioned the Bishop of Würzburg, Germany, to take up the process.

Dr. Paul Werner Scheele, Bishop of Würzburg, agreed and, on July 26, 1991, he, together with a group of Mariannhill Missionaries, three living blood-sisters of Father Engelmar, a few people from his former home village of Greifendorf, a small group of priests who had been in the concentration camp with Father Engelmar, the officials of the diocesan tribunal and many of Father Engelmar's admirers gathered in the crypt of the Pius Seminary in Würzburg, where Father Engelmar is buried, to open the beatification process.

After the service, all those officially involved in the process met for their first public session. The postulator read his document of appointment before the bishop and those assembled. Then the bishop and officials of the process took an oath of office orally and in writing. Records of the oaths were sealed solemnly and put in the files of the process.

Since then, the episcopal tribunal has heard the first witness of the process, Sister Huberta Unzeitig, C.P.S., a blood-sister of Father Engelmar.

Whoever receives favors through the intercession of Father Engelmar is asked to report them to one of the following addresses:

Postulator General	Postulator General
Mariannhill Missionaries	c/o Our Lady of Grace Monastery
Via S. Giovanni Eudes 91	23715 Ann Arbor Trail
00163 Rome, Italy	Dearborn Heights, MI 48127

Dearborn Heights, Michigan, U.S.A.
October 11, 1991

CHRONOLOGY

1875	Maria Unzeitig, née Kohl, Father Engelmar Unzeitig's mother, is born in Oberheinzendorf, Schönhengstgau (East Moravia), on August 22.
1879	Johann Unzeitig, father of Father Engelmar, comes into the world (August 18) in Pohler.
1911	Hubert (Father Engelmar) Unzeitig is born in Greifendorf near Zwittau on March 1 and baptized on March 4.
1914	Beginning of the First World War; Johann Unzeitig is drafted.
1916	Johann Unzeitig dies (January 14) of typhus in a Russian prison camp on the Volga.
1918	End of the War; the Sudetes Mountain areas are joined to Czechoslovakia, the inhabitants forced to become Czech citizens.
1920	Hubert Unzeitig celebrates his First Communion (May 16).
1921	Confirmation in Zwittau (September 26).
1925–26	Employment on a Czech farm (as hired hand).
1928	Secondary education as a late vocation in Reimlingen, Nördlingen.
1934	Matriculation, novitiate with Mariannhill in Holland.
1935	First profession, beginning of philosophical and theological studies in Würzburg.
1937	Regina (Sr. Adelhilde) Unzeitig, Father Engelmar's youngest sister, joins the Mariannhill Missionary Sisters of the Precious Blood in Wernberg, Carinthia.
1939	Ordination to the subdiaconate (February 19), diaconate (March 5), and priesthood (August 6); First Mass (August 15) in Greifendorf.

1940   Pastoral work in Riedegg, Austria, and Glöckelberg, Bohe-
        mian Forest.

1941   Arrest by the Gestapo (April 21) and "transfer" to the Da-
        chau concentration camp (June 3).

1943   Maria Unzeitig, Father Engelmar's mother, dies in
        Greifendorf.

1945   Father Engelmar volunteers for the typhus barracks in Da-
        chau, catches the disease and dies on March 2.
        Burial of the ashes, which had been smuggled out of the
        concentration camp, in the Würzburg municipal cemetery
        (Good Friday, March 30).

1946   Expulsion of all German-speaking Czechs; Father En-
        gelmar's relatives are evacuated.

1949   Maria (Sr. Huberta) Unzeitig becomes a Mariannhill Mis-
        sionary Sister in Neuenbeken.

1968   Transfer of the urn from the municipal cemetery to the
        Mariannhill church in Würzburg (November 20).

1985   Fortieth anniversary of death (March 2).

1986   Seventy-fifth birthday (March 1).

1989   Fiftieth anniversary of ordination (August 6).

ABBREVIATIONS FOR DOCUMENTS, ARCHIVES, MAGAZINES

GA   Generalate Archives of the Mariannhill Missionaries, Via S. Giovanni Eudes 91, 00163 Rome, Italy.

BAD   Letters from Dachau by Father Engelmar Unzeitig to his sister Maria-Huberta, June 1941–February 1945.

SvD   *Stimmen von Dachau (Römerbriefe)*, a publication of former Dachau priests 1946–1977, last edited by Father Heinz Römer, Neustadt a. d. Weinstrasse.

mmm   Mission magazine of the Mariannhill Missionaries (*Mariannhill*).

mmk   Mariannhill Mission Calendar.

FN   *Familiäre Nachrichten*, internal publication of the Mariannhill Missionaries.

FDA   Freiburg Diocesan Archives, Vol. 90, 1970.

GID   *Die Geistlichen in Dachau.* Standard work by Eugen Weiler (Mödling: St. Gabriel, 1971).

REFERENCES

We are giving only a small selection here. A more extensive listing of literature can be found in Adalbert L. Balling's book *Eine Spur der Liebe hinterlassen*, Missionsverlag Mariannhill, Würzburg/Reimlingen 1984, pp. 387–390.

Adam, Walter. *Nacht über Deutschland*. Vienna: Österreichischer Verlag, 1947.

Berger, Alexander. *Kreuz hinter Stacheldraht*. Bayreuth: Hestia, 1963.

Bernard, Jean. *Pfarrerblock 25 487*. Munich: Pustet, 1962.

Carls, Hans. *Dachau*. Cologne: Bachem, 1946.

Frank, Hans. *Im Angesicht des Galgens*. Göttingen: Plesse, 1955.

Frankl, Victor E. *Trotzdem Ja zum Leben sagen*. Munich: Kösel, 1977.

Goldschmitt, Franz. *Zeugen des Abendlandes*. Saarlouis: Felten, 1947.

Grün, Max von der. *Wie war das eigentlich?* Berlin-Neuwied: Luchterhand, 1981.

Haffner, Sebastian. *Anmerkungen zu Hitler*. Frankfurt: S. Fischer, 1981.

Hess, Sales. *Dachau—eine Welt ohne Gott*. Nürnberg: Sebaldus, 1946.

Höss, Rudolf. *Kommandant in Auschwitz*. Stuttgart: dva, 1958.

Joos, Josef. *Leben auf Widerruf*. Olten: Walter, 1946.

Kupfer-Koberwitz, Edgar. *Die Mächtigen und die Hilflosen*. 2 vols. Stuttgart: Vorwerk, 1957ff.

Lenz, Johannes Maria. *Christus in Dachau*. Published privately, Vienna, 1956.

Maser, Werner. *Das Regime*. Munich: Bertelsmann, 1983.

Michelet, Edmond. *Die Freiheitsstrasse*. Stuttgart: Europa Contact, 1960.

Münch, Maurus. *Unter 2579 Priestern in Dachau*. Trier: Zimmer, 1972.

Neuhäusler, Johann. *Wie war das im KZ Dachau?* Munich: Kuratorium für Sühnemal KZ Dachau, 1961.

―――. *Saat des Bösen*. Munich: Manz, 1964.

Picker, Henry. *Hitlers Tischgespräche*. Stuttgart: Seewald, 1963.

Pies, Otto. *Stephanus heute*. Kevelaer: Butzon & Bercker, 1957.

———. *Helfende Hände*. Freiburg i. Br.

Rost, Nico. *Goethe in Dachau*. Berlin: Volk und Welt, 1948.

Schnabel, Raimund. *Die Frommen in der Hölle*. Frankfurt: Röderberg, 1965.

Steinbock, Johann. *Das Ende von Dachau*. Salzburg: Österreichischer Kulturverlag, 1947.

Steinweder, Leonhard. *Christus im Konzentrationslager*. Salzburg: Müller, 1946.

Theek, Bruno. *Keller, Kanzel und Kaschott*. Berlin: Union, 1961.

Trenker, Luis. *Alles gut gegangen*. Munich: Bertelsmann, 1972.

Weiler, Eugen. *Die Geistlichen in Dachau*. Mödling: Sankt Gabriel, 1971.

Wiechert, Ernst. *Der Totenwald*. Munich: Desch, 1946.

Wilm, Ernst. *Dachau*. Dortmund-Hombruch: Evangelischer Verlags-Dienst, 1946.

———. *So sind wir nun Botschafter*. Bielefeld: Luther: 1979.

Zadek, Walter. *Sie flohen vor dem Hakenkreuz*. Hamburg: Rowohlt, 1981.

INDEX